THE STORY OF NOAH

Read, learn, pray, do the activities, and explore the story of Noah!

Meet the family

Noah was a good man. In fact, he was the only good man left in the whole world! God was angry with everyone else. The people who lived in his world were cruel to each other. They stole, lied, hurt each other, and forgot about the way God wanted them to live.

Noah was an old man. He had a wife and three grown-up sons. His sons were called Shem, Ham, and Japheth. Each of Noah's sons had a wife.

Noah trusted God. So when God asked Noah to do something very strange, he did it! God told him to build a huge boat called an ark. God planned to send a flood to wash the Earth clean. Only Noah and his family would survive. They would be safe inside the ark.

Genesis 6, verses 5 to 10

Something to think about:

God promised to save Noah's whole family. Imagine if your family was the only one left in the world!

Prayer:

Dear God, thank you for my family. Help me to do something kind for each one of them today. Amen.

Activity:

Noah had three sons. Can you name each one?

Which of these people are not part of Noah's family?

Is Noah going crazy?

God told Noah how to build the ark.

"Get some good strong wood to build the boat and cover it inside and out with tar. It needs to be 450 feet long, 75 feet wide, and 45 feet high. Put a roof on the top and build rooms inside. The boat should be three stories high. Put a door on one side. When the flood comes, you will be safe."

Noah did as God asked and built the ark. People watched and wondered. They even laughed at him! What was he doing building a boat so far from the sea?

Genesis 6, verses 11 to 18

Something to think about:

It's sometimes difficult to do the right thing. It's even harder when everyone else around you is doing something different and they laugh at you.

Prayer:

Help me, Lord God, to be brave enough to do what is good and right, even if others try to stop me.

Activity:

Noah used lots of tools to build the ark. Can you name these three tools?

Noah rounds up the animals

When God made the world, he had put all kinds of animals there to live. So God told Noah to bring animals, birds, and reptiles into the ark, male and female of every kind.

God told Noah to store up food to bring on board to feed them all.

God wanted there to be animals on the Earth after the flood too.

"I will send rain for forty days and nights," said God, "and a great flood will cover every living thing in the world."

Only Noah, his family, and the animals would be safe inside the ark.

Genesis 6, verses 19 to 22 and Genesis 7, verses 1 to 4

Something to think about:

Can you think why God told Noah to bring the animals into the ark?

Prayer:

Thank you, God, for animals. Help me to look after them and care for the creatures you have made.

Activity:

Can you find ten animals in the word box below?

- [ ] DONKEY
- [ ] ZEBRA
- [ ] ELEPHANT
- [ ] CHICKEN
- [ ] PIG
- [ ] SNAKE
- [ ] HORSE
- [ ] LION
- [ ] DOG
- [ ] CAMEL

Q	D	N	P	C	L	Z	P	C
W	E	C	Z	F	I	D	Z	A
A	I	H	D	I	O	O	D	M
R	p	I	G	E	N	G	D	E
A	L	C	F	R	S	R	O	L
Y	E	K	E	K	N	S	N	T
T	Z	E	B	R	A	M	K	C
W	Z	N	B	R	K	E	E	O
S	R	Y	F	I	E	Y	Y	E
S	C	I	J	H	O	R	S	E
Y	E	L	E	P	H	A	N	T
M	E	M	I	D	N	M	I	J

Getting ready to go

God told Noah to store up enough food to feed all the animals in the boat and enough for his own family, too. That was a lot of food!

Noah and his sons worked hard to prepare the ark for the flood. They collected food from the land and stored it on the ark. Then they stored up fresh water so there would be plenty to drink. When the flood came, there would be no more food to eat until it all grew again, fresh and new.

Genesis 7, verses 5 to 9

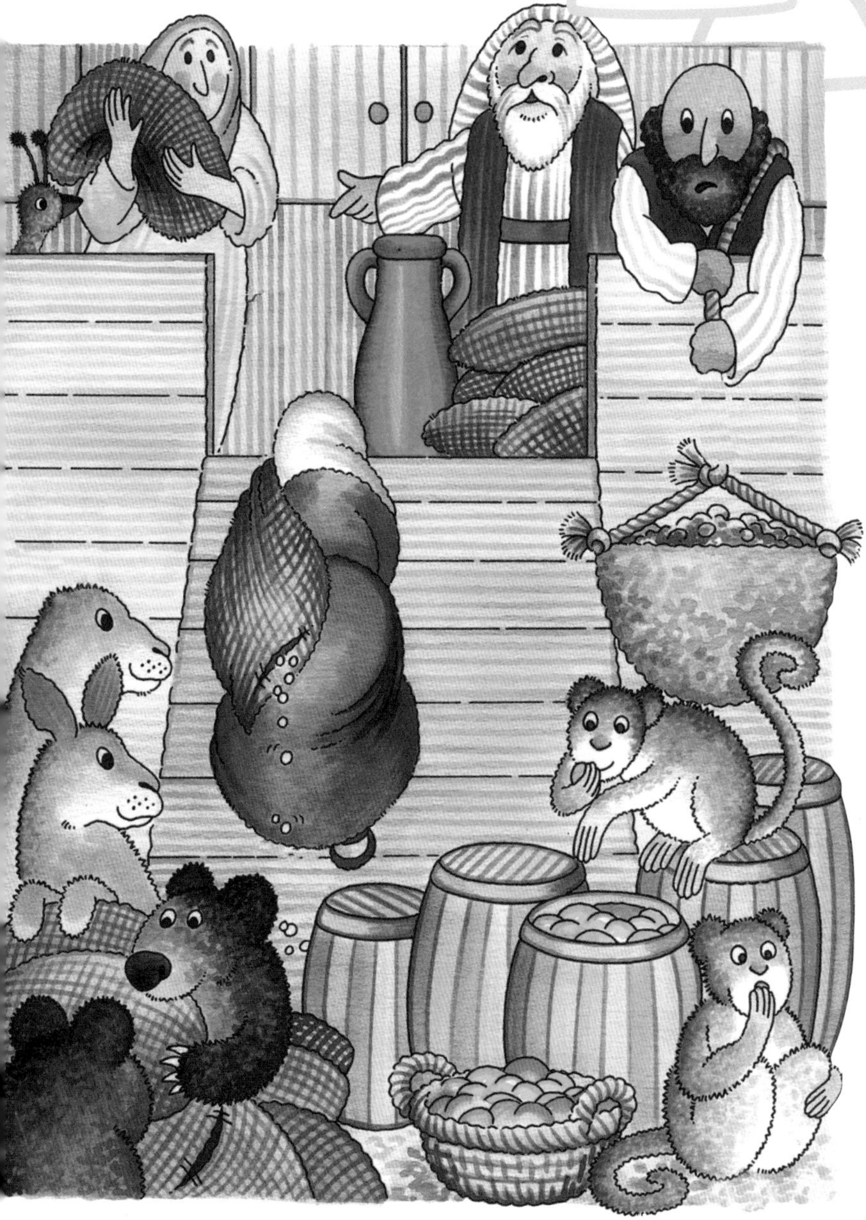

Something to think about:

What jobs did Noah and his family have to do before they were ready to leave?

Prayer:

Dear God, help me to be ready for the things you ask me to do.

Activity:

Can you spot ten differences between these pictures?

Saying goodbye

The ark was finished and Noah had done all that God asked him to do. Now Noah had to trust God for whatever would happen next.

Then it began to rain. First a few drops, then a steady stream started to fall. Noah and his wife went into the ark with their three sons and their wives. They took with them every kind of wild and tame animal, bird and reptile.

Noah and his family turned to say goodbye to everyone else on the land. They would never see them again.

When they were all in the ark, God closed the door tight. Soon the ark would begin to float on the waters.

Noah knew that God had promised to keep them safe.

Genesis 7, verses 10 to 16

Something to think about:

What would you want to take with you if you had to leave your home for ever? What would you miss most?

Prayer:

Help me to cope when things around me change, Lord, and to remember that you are with me wherever I go.

Activity:

Look at these shapes and patterns and guess which animals they belong to.

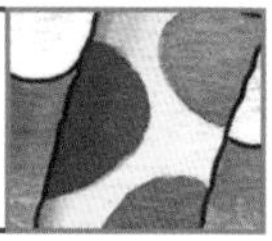

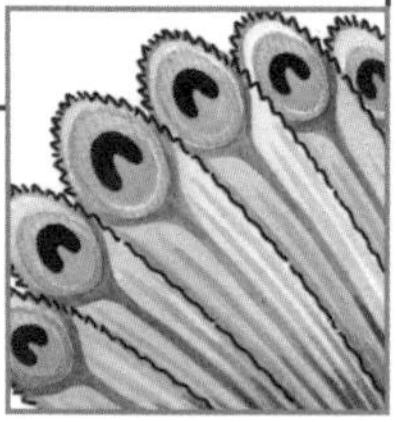

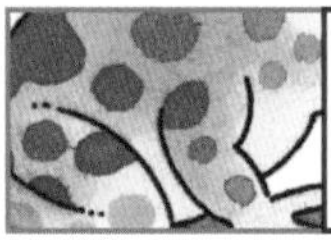

God's protection

The rain poured down for forty days and nights.

The ark started to float on the water. It bobbed about as the water got deeper.

Noah and his family could see the rain. Noah and his family heard the sound of the rain drumming on the roof. But the tar which Noah had painted on the ark kept the water out.

First the water covered the land, then it covered the trees. Soon even the mountain peaks were hidden by water!

Nothing was left alive except for Noah and his family and the animals in the ark. God kept them safe.

Then suddenly one day it was quiet. The rain had stopped.

Genesis 7, verses 17 to 23

Activity:

Can you find the eight picture fragments in the big picture?
Write the number of each fragment in the boxes provided.

Something to think about:

What are the things that frighten you?

Prayer:

Dear God, thank you for helping me when I am frightened.

Activity:

Can you complete the picture by adding the lightning and coloring in the sky?

Difficult times on board

The ark was smelly and noisy and uncomfortable with so many animals on board. But it was also the safest place to be.

Noah and his family made sure that all the animals had food to eat and water to drink. They also had to clear out all the smelly places to keep the ark clean. It kept them very busy!

They also waited...for the land to appear again when the water went down. It had rained for forty days and forty nights. It took another 150 days for the water to go down.

Then at last Noah could see the mountain tops.

Genesis 7, verse 24 and Genesis 8, verse 3

Something to think about:

What do you think was the worst thing about being in the ark for so long?

Prayer:

Dear God, please help me to be patient when I am finding things difficult.

Activity:

There are three different kinds of big cat in the picture. Can you name them?

Activity:

Can you complete the picture below?

Is there land out there?

When Noah could see the mountain tops again, he opened a window. He chose a raven from on board the ark and let it fly out through the window. The raven flew back and forth, but at first there was nowhere for it to settle. When the water had gone down, the raven did not return.

Then Noah sent out a dove to see if the Earth was dry yet. The dove could not find anywhere to land, so it flew back to Noah on the ark.

Seven days later, Noah sent the dove out again. This time it returned in the evening with a green olive leaf in its beak. There was land out there, and it was dry enough for the trees to flourish once more.

Noah waited seven more days, then sent the dove out again. This time it did not return. Noah knew that the Earth was safe again to live on.

Genesis 8, verses 4 to 12

Something to think about:

Noah had to wait many weeks before he found dry land. Can you think of a time when you had to wait patiently for something to happen?

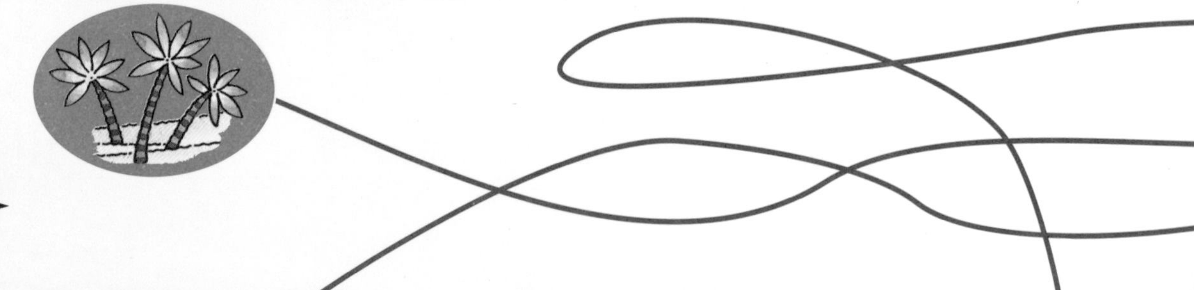

Prayer:

Dear God, please help me to wait patiently when I ask you for things. Thank you that you always hear my prayers.

Activity:

Follow these three paths to see which bird found dry land.

Thank you, God!

Now that Noah knew that the Earth must be dry, he made a hole in the roof of the ark and peered out. He could see that the land would soon be ready for them.

God called to Noah: "Leave the ark! Your wife, your sons and their wives, and all the animals and birds can come out at last and live on the Earth again."

So Noah came out, and all the creatures that had stayed on the ark for over a year came out too.

Then Noah built an altar to the Lord to say thank you for keeping them all safe.

Genesis 8, verses 13 to 20

Something to think about:

What can you thank God for today?

Prayer:

Dear God, thank you for my family, for food to eat and for your love and protection every day.

Activity:

Fill in the eight words to find two more special words.

1 ☐

2 ☐

3 ☐

4 ☐

5 ☐

6 ☐

7 ☐

8 ☐

Word clues:

1) It covered the land

2) Another type of large boat

3) Bump on the sea

4) Sea, sky and...

5) Noah's boat

6) Opposite of wet

7) Fluffy shape in the sky

8) It dried the land

A brand new start

"As long as the Earth remains," said God, "there will be planting and harvesting, cold and warm weather, winter and summer, day and night. I will bless you," said God to Noah. "I promise every living creature on the Earth that I will never again flood the Earth and destroy it. I have put a rainbow in the sky as a sign of my promise."

Genesis 8, verses 21 to 22 and Genesis 9, verses 9 to 17

Something to think about:

God made a promise to Noah. Can you think of any other promises God has made to his friends?

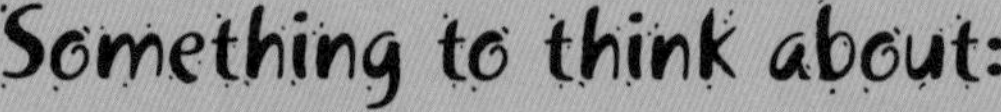

Prayer:

Dear God, thank you for all the good things you have given me.

Activity:

Color in the rainbow below and see if you can name all the colors.

R___ ___

O___ ___ ___ ___ ___

Y___ ___ ___ ___ ___

G___ ___ ___ ___

B___ ___ ___

I___ ___ ___ ___ ___

V___ ___ ___ ___ ___

God blesses the world

Noah and his sons farmed the land, and new plants and trees grew once more. Noah's sons moved away to farm different lands, and God blessed their wives with children. People began to live in the land again. The animals spread across the Earth and had babies and lived where they could find food. Life began again on the Earth. Noah planted a vineyard and was happy in the new land God gave him. He died when he was a very old man.

Genesis 9, verses 18 to 20 and verses 28 to 29

Something to think about:

If you were Noah, what would you do first after the flood?

Prayer:

Dear God, thank you that you have plans for my life, too.

Activity:

Noah planted a vineyard. Can you color in the dotted pieces of this picture to see how many grapes there are in the bunch?

Activity:

Can you name these fruits?

THE STORY OF
JOSEPH
Read, learn, pray, do the activities,
and explore the story of Joseph!

Joseph and his brothers

Activity:
How many differences can you find between these pictures of Jacob and his sons?

Jacob had a very large family. He had twelve sons and a daughter. He lived with his family in the land of Canaan.

Jacob's sons were called Reuben, Simeon, Levi, Judah, Issachar, Zebulun, Dan, Naphtali, Gad, Asher, Joseph and Benjamin, the youngest son. Out of all his sons, Jacob loved Joseph most of all. Joseph was Jacob's favorite son.

Jacob's sons looked after his sheep and goats. Joseph brought reports to his father about how well or badly his brothers were working. They didn't like it when Joseph told their father they had not been working well!

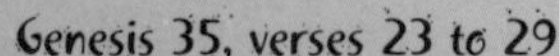
Genesis 35, verses 23 to 29

Something to think about:

How would you feel if you were one of Joseph's brothers?

Prayer:

Dear God, thank you for my family. Help us to be kind to each other and remember that each one in the family is special.

Joseph's wonderful coat

Activity:

Can you design a colorful coat for Joseph?

When Joseph was seventeen years old, his father Jacob gave him a very special gift. He gave him a wonderful new coat to wear.

Joseph was very proud of his new coat. He strutted around in front of all his brothers, saying, "Look at me! Look what Dad has bought for me!"

But Joseph's brothers were jealous.

"Why does Dad love Joseph more than us?" they muttered. "Why haven't we been given robes like that?" they grumbled.

Joseph didn't seem to hear them. He thought only about his handsome coat.

Genesis 37, verses 2 to 4

Something to think about:

Was it fair for Jacob to give only Joseph a special gift?

Prayer:

Dear God, thank you for special gifts I receive from my family and from you. Help me to be grateful for everything I have.

Activity:

Joseph's coat was very colorful. What do you get if you mix the following colors? Fill in the shape with the right color.

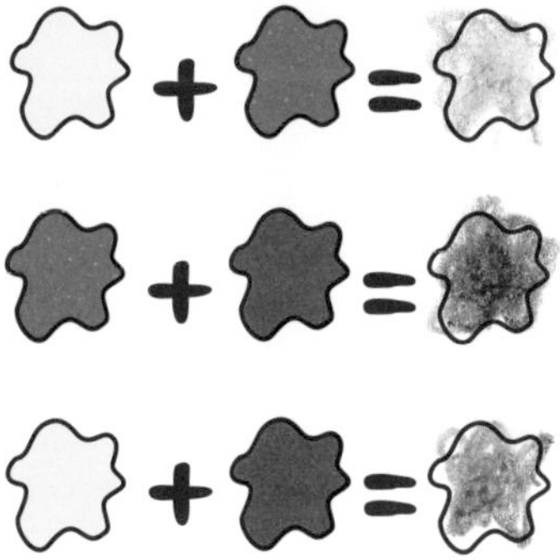

+ =

+ =

+ =

Joseph has strange dreams

One night, Joseph had a very strange dream. He dreamed that he and his brothers were tying up sheaves of corn in a field. Suddenly his sheaf of corn stood up straight and the eleven other sheaves of corn all bowed down to his sheaf.

Joseph's brothers were angry. "Do you think you will rule over us?" they scoffed.

Another night Joseph dreamed he saw eleven stars, the sun and the moon, all bowing down to him!

Joseph told his father about the dream. Jacob said, "What is this? Do you think that your mother and I and your brothers will bow down before you?"

Joseph's brothers were very jealous.

Genesis 37, verses 5 to 11

Activity:

Can you rearrange the letters to discover what Joseph dreamed about?

RATSS	

Something to think about:

Do you think Joseph should have kept quiet about his dreams?

1

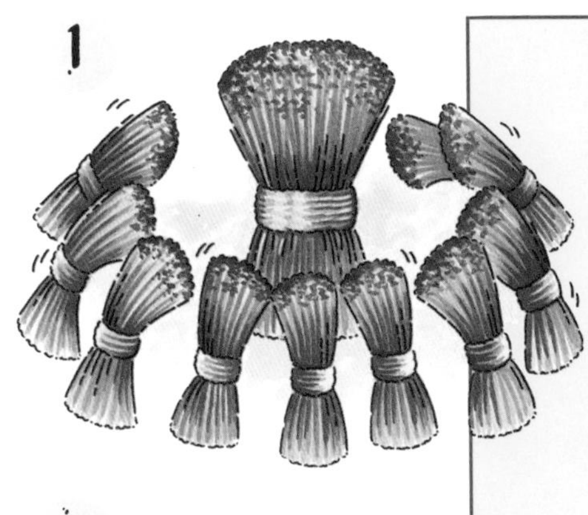

2

3

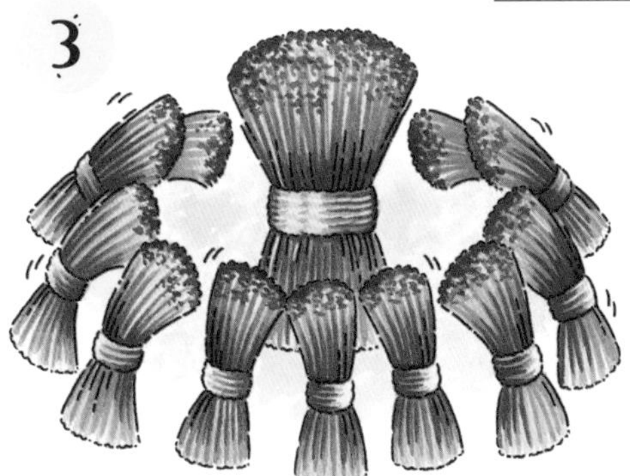

Activity:

Find the two dream pictures that show the same number of sheaves and stars as Joseph had brothers. Put the number for each picture in the boxes below.

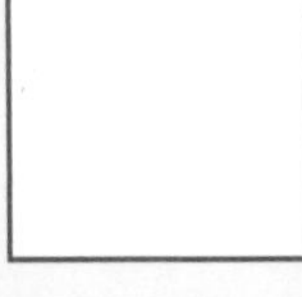

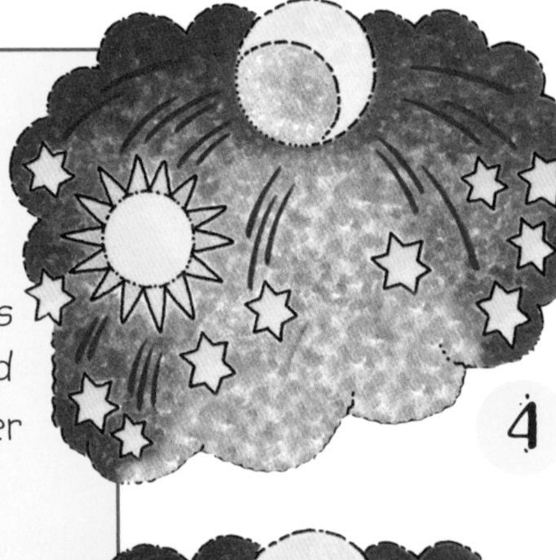

4

5

Prayer:

Dear God, help me to think before I speak so that I don't make other people sad.

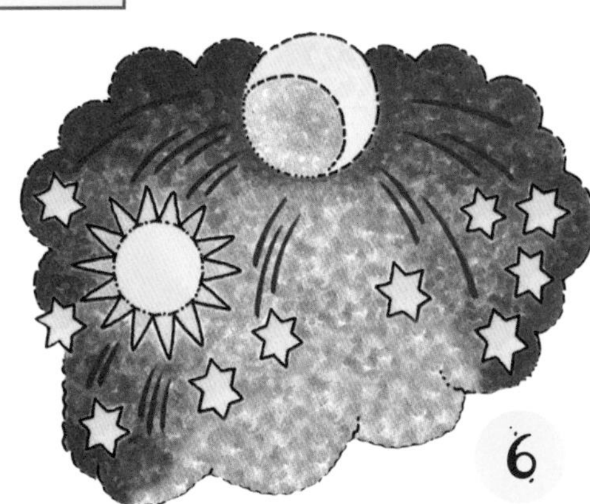

6

Joseph's brothers are jealous

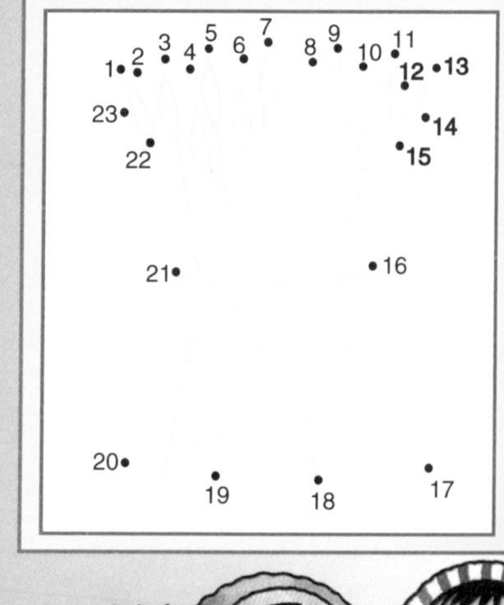

Joseph's brothers were very angry with Joseph.

First, he had told their father that they were not working hard enough in the fields with the sheep. Then, their father had given Joseph a fine robe to show that he was their dad's favorite! That made them feel left out.

To make matters even worse, Joseph had started telling them about his strange dreams, in which he was somehow better than his brothers. They were just old corn stacks and fading stars. Why did Joseph think he was so much more important?

The brothers now hated Joseph. They wanted to get rid of him.

Genesis 37, verses 1 to 11

Activity:

Join up the dots to complete this picture.

Something to think about:

Joseph's brothers became so jealous that they hated Joseph. What makes you jealous of other people?

Prayer:

Dear God, I'm sorry for times when I have been jealous of others, and when I haven't been kind to them.

Activity:

Which of these are brothers of Joseph? Write yes or no in the boxes.

Joseph is sold to be a slave

Prayer:
Dear God, please help me to remember that Jesus is always my friend, even if other people are not being friendly.

One day when the brothers were all out in the fields looking after the sheep, they thought up a cruel plan to get rid of Joseph. "Let's throw the dreamer into a well and leave him there to die! We'll tell Dad that a wild animal got him," they plotted.

So when Joseph came to see them, they tore off his fine robe and threw him into an empty well! But a group of travelling traders came past. They were on their way to Egypt. The brothers quickly changed their plan and sold Joseph to the traders. He was taken away as a slave!

The brothers told their father that Joseph had been killed by a wild animal. Jacob tore his clothes and was heartbroken.

Genesis 37, verses 23 to 36

Something to think about:
Joseph was saved from dying in the well. God had a plan for Joseph's life.

Activity: Can you find six words that describe Joseph's brothers?

Q	R	T	A	L	I	A	R	S	F	P
W	B	H	S	R	I	B	N	S	S	Y
A	Y	O	A	N	G	R	Y	J	S	S
	F	M	D	I	C	R	U	E	L	E
				T	O		R	A	Y	L
								L	M	F
							H	O	E	I
							G	U	E	S
							D	S	H	H
							R	Z	A	P
							E	I	P	L

Joseph works for Potiphar

Joseph was taken to Egypt, where he was sold as a slave to Potiphar, the captain of the palace guard. God looked after Joseph.

Joseph worked hard in Potiphar's home and everyone liked him. Potiphar put Joseph in charge of his household. God blessed Potiphar's household when Joseph was in charge. God helped Joseph to do well at his job.

One day, things changed. Potiphar's wife told lies about Joseph and said he had tried to hurt her. Potiphar was furious and threw Joseph into jail. But God was with Joseph there too. Joseph had done nothing wrong.

Genesis 39, verses 1 to 21

Something to think about:

God helped Joseph to do well at his work. God blessed the people around him.

Prayer:

Dear God, when things don't go quite as I expect, please help me to trust you. Thank you that you are always with me.

Activity:

Only six of the picture details below were taken from the pictures on this page. Can you mark them with a checkmark, and put an X next to the two that don't come from this page?

Joseph in jail

Joseph was thrown into jail where the King's prisoners were kept. But very soon the warden of the jail began to like Joseph. He gave him jobs to do. Joseph did well because God was helping him.

It wasn't long before the warden decided to put Joseph in charge of the other prisoners. The warden trusted him.

In jail, Joseph met the King's chief baker and the King's wine steward. One night they both had very strange dreams which troubled them. They asked Joseph to help them.

Genesis 39, verses 19 to 23; chapter 40, verses 1 to 8

Something to think about:

God was always with Joseph, even in jail when he didn't know if he'd ever be free again.

Activity:

Which prisoner was the wine steward, which one was the King's baker, and which one was a shepherd? You can write the answers above each prisoner.

Prayer:
Dear God, please be with people in jail, especially those who have done nothing wrong, or who are in jail for being Christians.

Joseph understands dreams

Joseph asked the wine steward and the baker to tell him their dreams.

The wine steward spoke first: "I saw a grapevine with three branches. The grapes became ripe and I squeezed them into the King's cup and gave it to him to drink." Joseph told him that in three days he would be freed from jail.

The baker spoke next, but his dream did not end happily. "I was carrying three baskets of cakes and pastries, when some birds swooped down and ate them all up!" said the baker.

Joseph looked sad. "I'm sorry to say you will never be free. The King means to kill you in three days!"

Three days later, the dreams came true, just as Joseph had said!

Genesis 40, verses 1 to 23

Something to think about:

God helped Joseph to understand dreams. Can you think of anyone else in the Bible who had strange dreams?

Prayer:

Dear God, please be with me in my dreams and through each night.

Activity:

To re-create this picture the squares have to be put in the correct place, Can you put the correct position number in each circle?

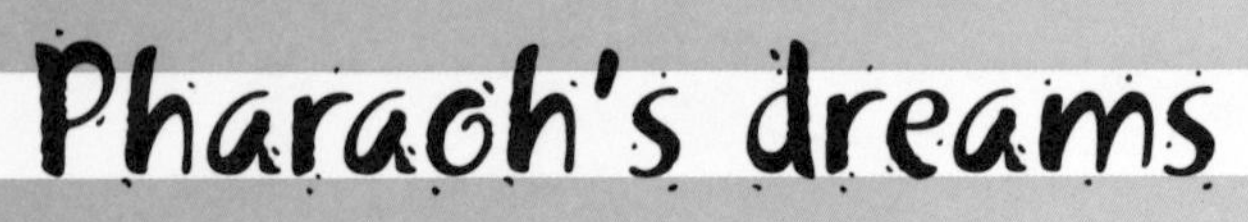

Pharaoh's dreams

Two whole years later, the King of Egypt had two strange dreams. The wine steward, whom Joseph had helped in jail, suddenly remembered Joseph and told the King about him. Joseph washed and shaved himself and was brought before the great King of Egypt.

"Your majesty, tell me your dreams!" said Joseph.

"I was standing on the river bank when seven fat cows came out of the river to feed. Then seven thin cows came and ate them all up! But they stayed as thin as before! Then I dreamed I saw seven fat ears of corn, which were eaten up by seven thin ears of corn! What does this mean?"

Joseph told the King that there would be a time of great famine in the land. He must store up food for seven years to feed the people when there was no food for the seven following years.

The King was delighted and put Joseph in charge of storing food for Egypt.

Genesis 41, verses 1 to 43

Something to think about:

Joseph went from being a prisoner to being the King's special governor. What a turnaround!

Activity:

The King counted the cows in his dream. Can you find the answers to these strange sums?

=1 =2 =3

=4 =5 =6

=7 =8 =9

\+ =

− + =

\+ − =

You could write your answers with numbers or draw the symbol that represents the answer.

Prayer: Dear God, thank you that you have a plan for my life, too.

Joseph sees his brothers again

The famine spread to countries all over the region. There was no food in Canaan where Joseph's family still lived. So one day Jacob sent his sons to Egypt to ask for food.

In Egypt the brothers did not recognise their brother Joseph. Joseph now looked very important with a gold chain from the King round his neck. The brothers bowed low before him and begged for food.

At first, Joseph wanted to test them to see whether they had changed their ways. He saw that they were very sorry for what they had done. Eventually he told them who he was. They were frightened in case he was still angry, but Joseph forgave them.

Genesis 42 to 45

Prayer:

Dear God, help me to forgive people when they say sorry, just as you forgive me.

Activity:

You can color in this picture of Joseph. Would Joseph's brothers recognise him from your picture?

Something to think about:

Joseph's brothers bowed down to him. Can you remember what Joseph had seen in his dreams?

Joseph sees his father again

Joseph sent his brothers back to Canaan to get Jacob, their father.

"Joseph is alive! He's in Egypt!" they told him excitedly. "In fact, he is ruler of Egypt!" Jacob could hardly believe it. His beloved son was alive!

Joseph had sent carts to bring Jacob and their family back to Egypt.

God spoke to Jacob in a dream, telling him not to be afraid to go to Egypt. "I will go with you," promised God.

So Jacob made the journey, and Joseph came out to meet him. He threw his arms around his father's neck and wept tears of joy.

Jacob stayed in Egypt with Joseph to the end of his days. The King allowed them all to live in the land, and Joseph made sure they always had enough food. God blessed Joseph's family.

Genesis 46 to 47, verse 12

Activity:

Can you help Jacob find the way to Joseph?

Something to think about:

Jacob thought he would never see Joseph again. But God surprised him!

Prayer:

Dear God, thank you for all that you give us, and that you sometimes give us lovely surprises too!

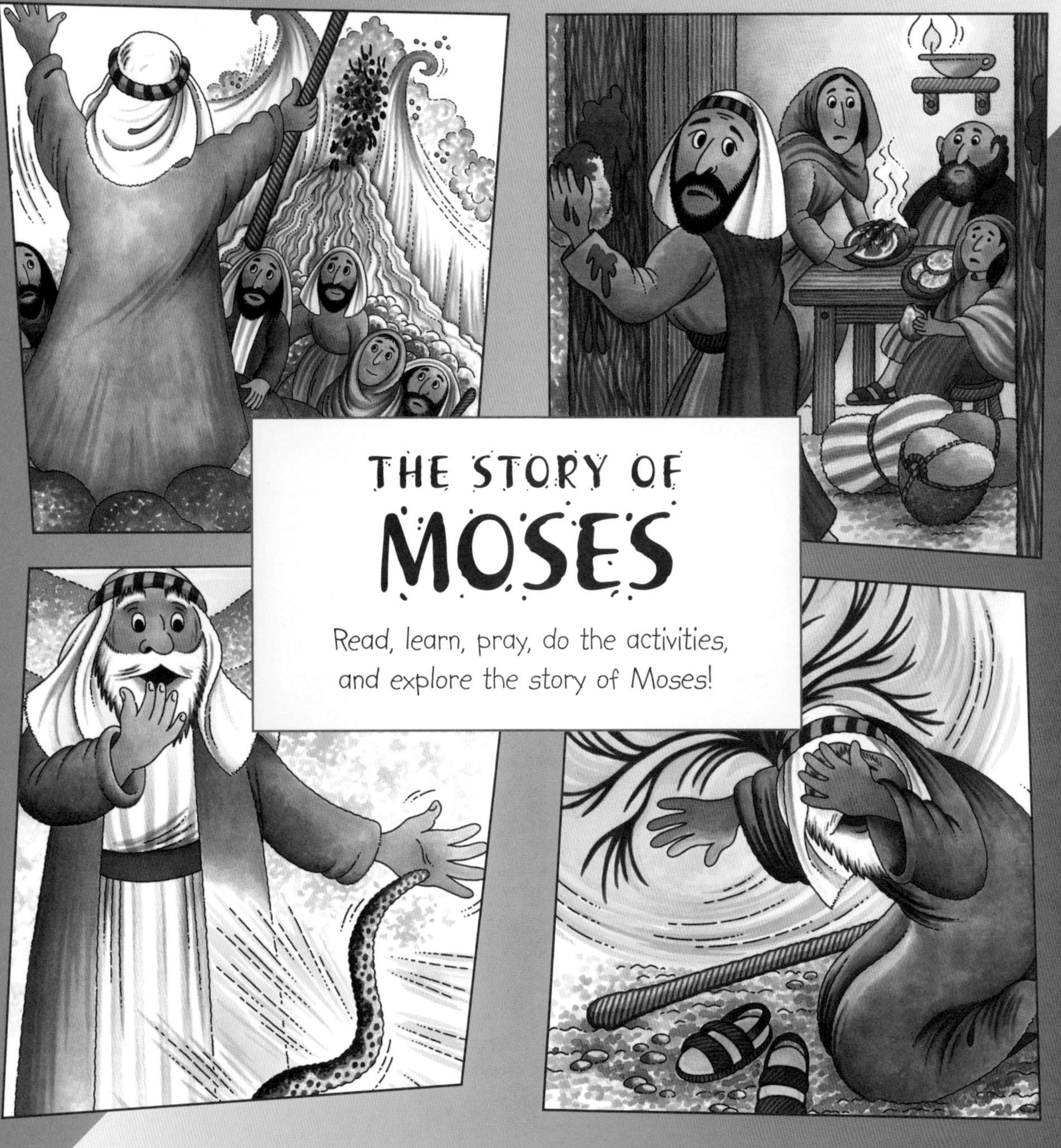
THE STORY OF
MOSES
Read, learn, pray, do the activities,
and explore the story of Moses!

Moses is hidden in a basket

Moses was born in Egypt. Pharaoh, the King of Egypt, gave a cruel command to drown all the Israelite baby boys in the Nile River.

Moses' mother had a plan to save her little son. She made a basket and coated it with tar. She placed her baby in the basket and hid it among the reeds in the river. The baby's sister, Miriam, watched from behind the reeds.

Pharaoh's daughter, the royal princess, came to the river to bathe. She heard crying from the basket, opened the lid and lifted up the baby.

Miriam stepped out from behind the reeds. "Shall I go get an Israelite woman to nurse the baby?" she asked.

So Miriam went and got her own mother! Moses' mother nursed him until he was old enough to go and live in the royal palace as the princess' adopted son.

Exodus 2, verses 1 to 10

Activity:

Can you put *baby* Moses in the *basket*?
You can draw the *baby* and color him in.

Prayer:

Dear God, thank you for all the people who looked after me when I was a *baby* and helped me to grow strong.

Activity:

There is only one hidden *basket* shape like this. Can you find it?

Something to think about:

God protected Moses when he was a tiny *baby*. God provided people to love him and look after him.

Moses runs away

Activity:

Where did Moses run away to? Can you get there and write the name in the box?

a b c

When Moses grew up, he often watched his own Israelite people working as slaves for Pharaoh. He saw how cruelly they were treated.

One day, he saw an Egyptian hitting a slave very hard. Moses was furious. He looked to see if anyone was watching, then he stepped forward and killed the Egyptian. He buried him in the sand.

The next day, Moses saw two slaves fighting and asked why they were hurting each other. One of them said, "Are you going to kill me now, like you killed that Egyptian yesterday?"

Moses was terrified. Someone had seen him after all. Moses ran away, far from Pharaoh's palace, to a land called Midian.

Exodus 2, verses 11 to 25

Something to think about:

Moses thought no one had seen the bad thing he had done. But they had, and God had seen it too.

Prayer:

Dear God, please help me to tell the truth and not hide from you the wrong things I do.

Welcome to

___ ___ ___ ___ ___ ___

Moses and the burning bush

Put a circle around the two shoes that belong to Moses.

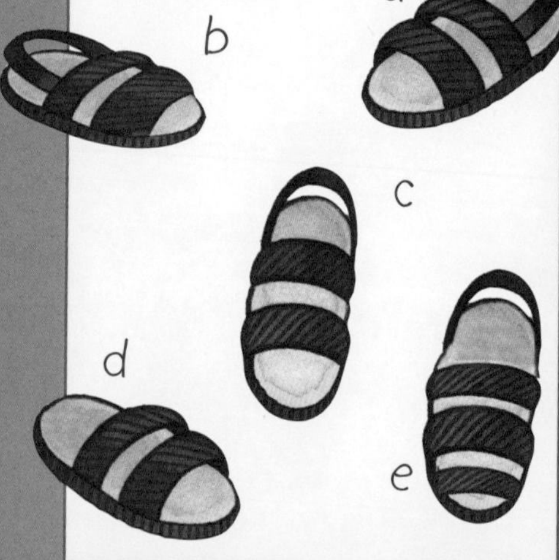

Something to think about:

God appeared to Moses in an unexpected place – a burning bush!

Moses lived in Midian for forty years. He married Zipporah and had a son.

Moses looked after Zipporah's father's sheep and goats, leading them across the desert places and mountains to find grass and water.

One day, when Moses was looking after the sheep at Horeb, the mountain of God, he saw an amazing sight.

There was a burning bush in front of him which did not burn up.

God called to Moses from within the bush: "Moses! Moses!"

Moses stepped closer to the bush.

"Take off your sandals," said God. "You are standing on holy ground." At once, Moses covered his eyes.

"I am the God of your father, the God of Abraham, the God of Isaac, and the God of Jacob," said God. "I have seen my people suffering. I am sending you to Pharaoh to bring my people out of Egypt."

Exodus 3, verses 1 to 22

Activity:
Color in this picture of Moses and the burning bush.

Prayer:
Dear God, help me to be ready to listen to you wherever I am.

"I can't do it!"

God told Moses to go to Pharaoh and ask him to let the Israelite slaves go free. God told Moses to tell the Israelites that he would be their leader.

But Moses was worried. "What if no one listens to me?" he said.

"Look at the staff in your hand," said God. "Throw it to the ground."

At once the staff became a snake!

When Moses took the snake by the tail, it turned back into a staff.

"But I am not very good at speaking," said Moses.

"I will help you," said God.

"But I can't do it!" said Moses. "Please send someone else!"

God became angry with Moses.

"Your brother, Aaron, can help you. I will help you both," said God.

Exodus 3, verses 7 to 9 and chapter 4, verses 1 to 17

Activity:
Can you draw a pattern on the snake and color it in?

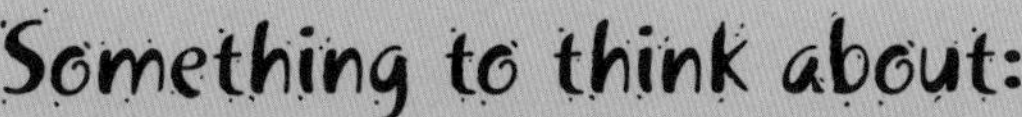

Something to think about:

Moses thought he wasn't clever enough to do what God wanted. But God wouldn't take no for an answer!

Prayer:

Dear God, help me to be willing to do the things you ask me. Help me this week to...

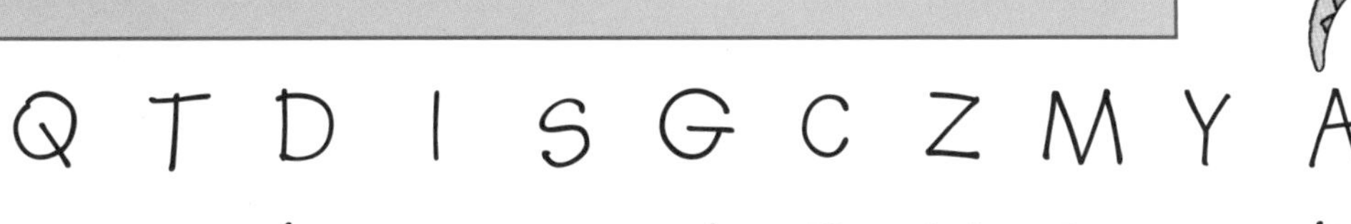

Q	T	D	I	S	G	C	Z	M	Y	A
W	A	P	Y	T	H	O	N	R	S	P
A	O	R	D	N	R	B	F	A	G	L
R	M	W	O	U	E	R	S	T	R	P
B	A	I	U	J	C	A	D	T	A	G
Y	R	T	B	R	S	P	F	L	S	A
F	A	D	D	E	R	O	Y	E	S	C

Activity:

Can you find five snakes in the word search?

Moses goes to see Pharaoh

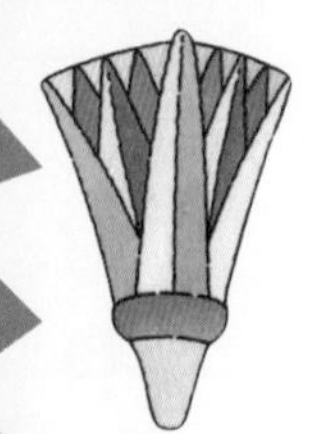

Moses and his brother Aaron went to see Pharaoh.

"God says, let my people go!" they said boldly.

But Pharaoh replied, "Who is your God? I do not know him. I shall not let the people go."

Pharaoh became even more cruel to the Israelite slaves. They made bricks from straw and mud. Now Pharaoh made them find their own straw. This made them work very slowly.

"You are all very lazy!" said Pharaoh.

The Israelite men in charge of the slaves became angry with Moses and Aaron. "You have just made things worse for us all!" they shouted.

But Moses and Aaron told them what God had said. God promised to set them free. Moses and Aaron believed it, even though the other Israelites would not listen.

Exodus 5, verses 1 to 23

Prayer:

Dear God, thank you that you can see the big picture and your plans for my life. Help me to trust you more.

Something to think about:

Things did not go quite as Moses planned. He obeyed God, but for a time things seemed to get worse!

Activity:

Draw a line to connect each detail to the right spot in the picture.

Activity:

Draw a circle around the four symbols that are exactly the same as symbols on the far left.

The plagues of Egypt

Pharaoh would not listen to the cry of the Israelites. Moses and Aaron tried to persuade him to let the people go. They even performed miracles.

Then God told Moses to stretch out his staff over the Nile River. The water turned to blood! The Egyptians were unable to drink the water any more or bathe in it.

Something to think about:
Why do you think Pharaoh would not let the Israelite people go?

Next, God sent a plague of frogs. Frogs hopped into everyone's house and bed, even into the royal palace.

Then came a plague of gnats, then flies, which filled the Egyptians' houses.

Another plague fell upon the land. This time all the cows and sheep died. Then all the Egyptians were covered in boils and their skin became terribly sore. Still Pharaoh wouldn't budge.

A plague of hailstones hit the land, then locusts came and devoured the crops. Darkness fell upon the land and no one could see.

But the final plague was the most terrible of all. Moses warned Pharaoh that all the firstborn children of Egypt would die in a night.

Exodus 7 to 11

Prayer:

Dear God, thank you that you are very powerful and that you are on my side in times of trouble.

What was the name of the river that turned to blood?

How many plagues were there all together?

Activity:

Can you number these six plagues in the right order?

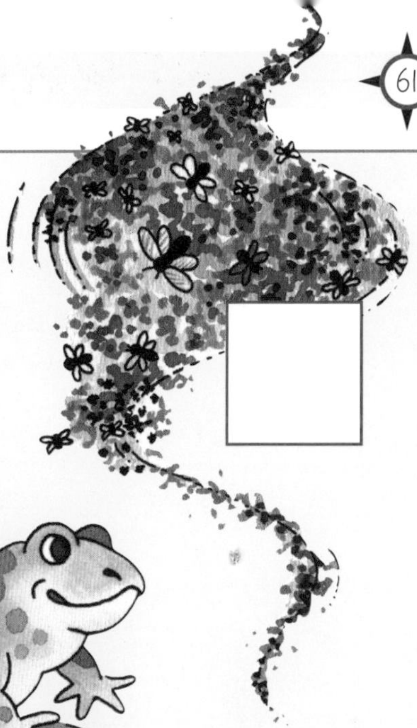

The Passover meal

God told Moses to tell all the Israelites to get ready. They must each take a lamb, kill it, and put some of the lamb's blood on the doorposts of the house. They must then roast the lamb over a fire and eat the meat, with bitter herbs and bread made without yeast. This was to be called the Passover.

That night, death came to Egypt. All the firstborn sons and animals of the Egyptians died.

Even Pharaoh's son died. There was terrible wailing in the land.

Death passed over all the homes of the Israelites, but not one was harmed. God saved them all.

Pharaoh called Moses and Aaron. "Go!" he said. "Leave Egypt! Take your animals and go, as you asked."

The final terrible plague made Pharaoh change his mind. He let the people go.

Exodus 12, verses 1 to 32

Activity:

There are eight things that are missing from this picture. Can you find all the changes?
Draw an arrow from each number to a change.

1

2

3

4

5

6

7

8

Something to think about:

God told his people to remember the Passover forever.

Can you think of a way in which your church celebrates how God saved his people?

Prayer:

Dear God, you kept the Israelites safe during the Passover because they were your special people. Thank you that I am special to you, too.

Crossing the Red Sea

God led the Israelites out of Egypt. He went ahead of them in a pillar of cloud by day, and a pillar of fire at night. God led them to the Red Sea.

Pharaoh, meanwhile, suddenly changed his mind about letting the Israelites go! He sent soldiers on horses and in chariots to chase after them.

Something to think about:
The Israelites thought they were trapped, but God saved them in an amazing way!

Moses told his people not to be afraid, even though Pharaoh's troops were coming nearer and nearer!

Moses stretched his staff over the water of the Red Sea. The water parted! The Israelites passed through the Red Sea on dry land and reached the other side.

Pharaoh's soldiers tried to follow, but Moses raised his staff over the water again, and the sea came crashing down. All the Egyptians were drowned.

When the Israelites saw how powerful God was, they put their trust in him and believed what Moses said.

Exodus 14, verses 1 to 31

Prayer:

Lord, you can do amazing things! Please help me when I face danger or scary situations like...

Activity:

Can you find these faces in the crowd? Put a number in each box to identify each face. Which face is not in the crowd?

Manna and quail

"Where's the food?" grumbled the Israelites.

God had guided them across the Red Sea to safety on the other side, away from Egypt and Pharaoh at last. But now the Israelites were grumbling. And their stomachs were rumbling...

"I will send bread from heaven for you," said God to Moses.

"The people must go out and gather enough for one day at a time. On the sixth day of the week, they must bring in twice as much as on the other days, so that they can rest on the seventh day."

That evening, quail flew over the camp and the people caught them.

In the morning, dew covered the ground. When it had gone, there were flakes of white manna on the ground. It was the bread from heaven which God had sent. It tasted like wafers made with honey.

God had provided for all their needs once again.

Exodus 16, verses 1 to 36

Something to think about:

Why do you think that God told the people to collect enough food for one day at a time?

Activity:

What is missing from this picture?

Activity:

What's wrong with this picture?

Activity:

Can you copy this picture of a quail? Use the grid to help.

Prayer:

Dear God, thank you for giving me food each day. Help me to remember that all I have comes from you.

The Ten Commandments

Moses went up Mount Sinai to talk to God.

"You know what I have done for you," said God. "I have carried you on eagle's wings and brought you to myself. Obey me and my commandments and I will make Israel into a great nation, my most special nation in the whole earth. I will make a covenant with you."

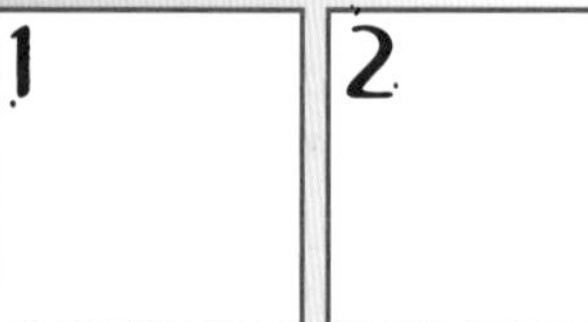

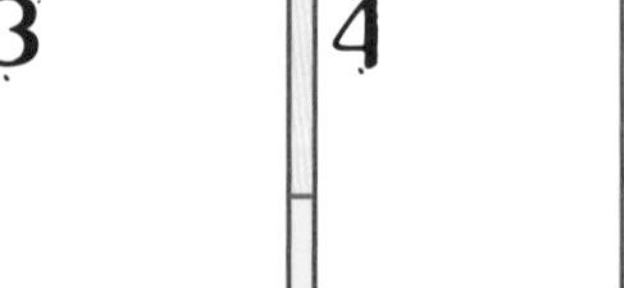

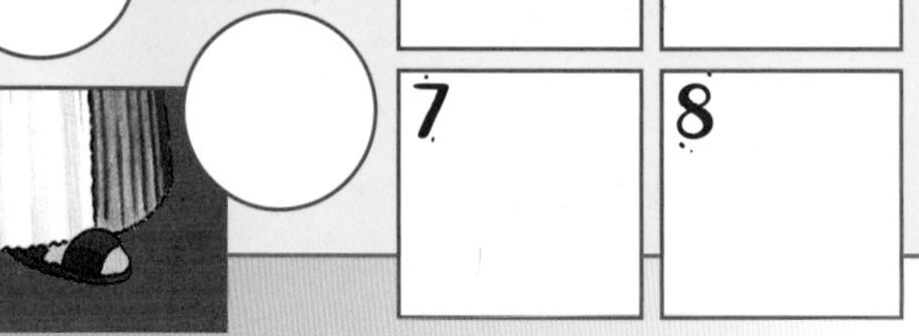

1	2
3	4
5	6
7	8

Activity:

To re-create this picture the squares have to be put in the correct place, Can you put the correct position number in each circle?

God gave Moses laws called the Ten Commandments:

"I am the Lord your God. Have no other gods besides me.

Do not make statues or anything else to worship.

Do not use my name carelessly.

Remember to keep the seventh day holy.

Do not work on this day.

Respect your father and mother.

Do not murder anyone.

Do not be unfaithful to your wife or husband.

Do not steal.

Do not tell lies about anyone.

Do not look greedily at things other people have got."

There was thunder and lightning and a trumpet blast. The laws were written on stone tablets.

Exodus 19 to 20

Activity:

God gave Moses ten laws. Color in the shapes with a red dot to see how the Romans wrote ten.

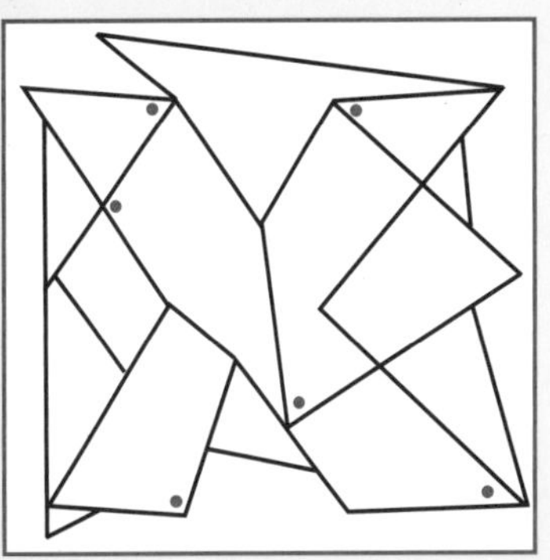

Something to think about:

Think about the Ten Commandments which God gave to Moses. Which ones do you find hard to keep?

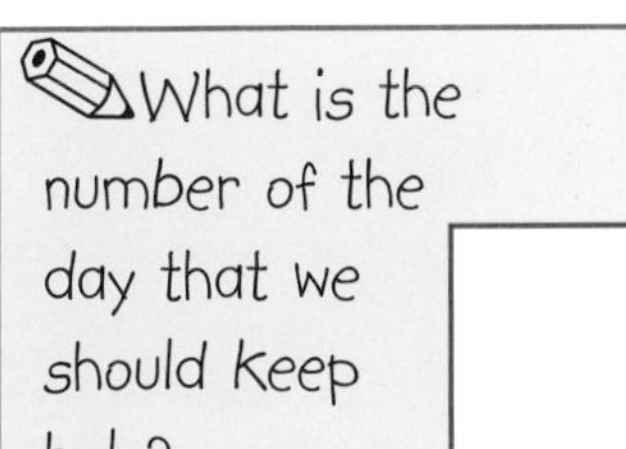

What is the number of the day that we should keep holy?

Prayer:

Dear God, help me to remember that you are very holy. Help me to live in a way which pleases you.

The Promised Land

God promised to lead the Israelites to a new land flowing with milk and honey.

It took many years to reach the land which God had promised. On the way there, God spoke to Moses many times. He told Moses to build the tabernacle – a holy place where people would worship God. Aaron was made a high priest. Special objects were made for the tabernacle: a golden lampstand and the ark of the Covenant. This was a sacred box which contained the stone tablets with the laws God gave to Moses on Mount Sinai.

When Moses was a very old man, God took him to the top of a mountain. From there he could see a new land in the distance. It was the promised land!

But Moses never set foot there. He died. God chose Joshua to continue the journey.

Deuteronomy 34 and Joshua 1

Something to think about:

Do you remember how Moses had been afraid to lead the people of Israel when God first asked him? Think of ways in which God helped him.

Activity:
Can you find your way to the promised land?

Prayer:
Dear God, please help me to trust you when I have something difficult to do. I know that you are always able to help me.

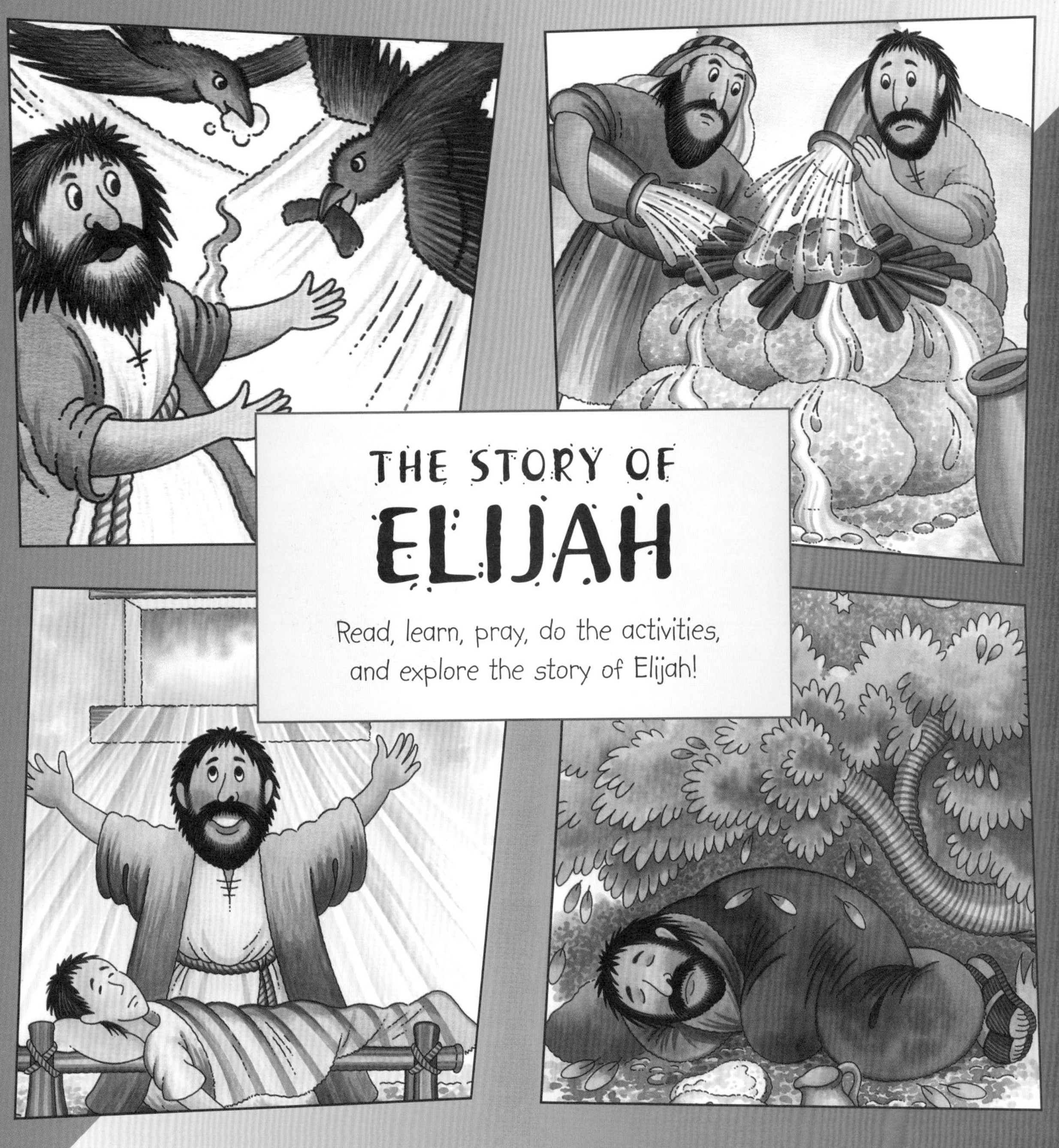

THE STORY OF ELIJAH

Read, learn, pray, do the activities, and explore the story of Elijah!

Elijah speaks to the king

Elijah was a prophet. God often spoke to him and Elijah listened. God told him to give messages to the people of Israel.

At this time Israel was ruled by King Ahab. There had been many kings of Israel before, some good and some bad. Ahab was one of the bad kings.

God gave Elijah a message for the king. Elijah knew he must go to King Ahab and speak firmly.

"Ahab!" said Elijah. "There is going to be a terrible drought. There will be no rain for many years. It will only come when God gives the word."

1 Kings 17, verse 1

Prayer:

Dear God, please help me listen when you speak to me and do the things you want me to.

Something to think about:

God talks to those who want to listen to him.

Activity:

Can you help Elijah find his way to the king?

Elijah hides from Ahab

Elijah knew he was in danger. King Ahab and his wife didn't like what God's prophets were saying. So they were trying to kill them! God told Elijah to run away and hide near Cherith Brook. God would provide everything that Elijah needed.

"I have ordered ravens to feed you," said God.

Sure enough, ravens brought Elijah bread and meat every morning and evening. Elijah drank the cool water from the brook until it dried up.

1 Kings 17, verses 2 to 6

Something to think about:

If we trust God, he will provide us with all the things we need.

Prayer:

Dear God,
thank you for
giving me
food to eat.

Activity:

God kept Elijah alive. Fill in the blanks with the letters e or a to find four things that God sent to keep Elijah alive.

w		t		r	
r		v		n	s
b	r			d	
m			t		

Activity: Which raven delivered food to Elijah?

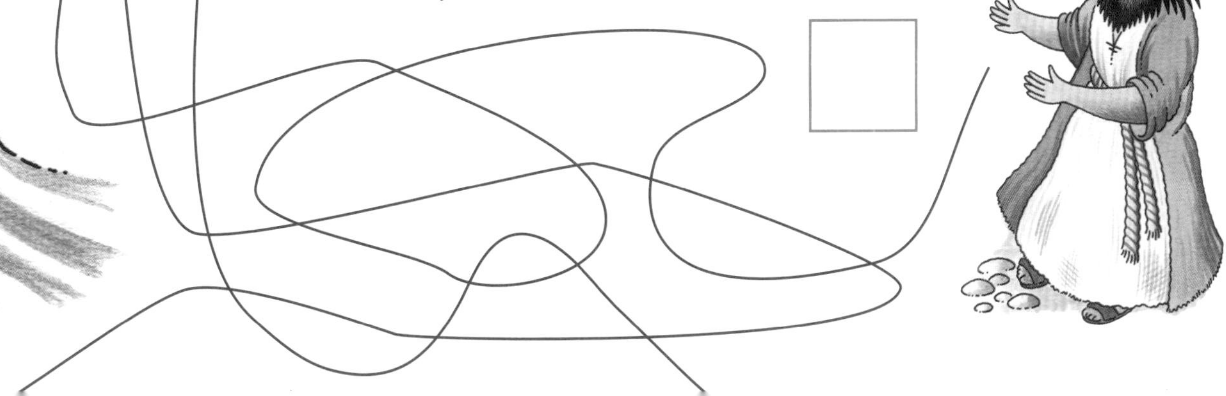

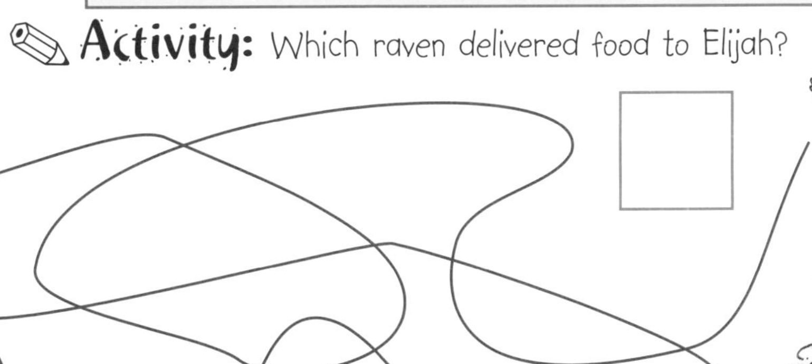

A widow helps Elijah

God told Elijah to go to Zarephath, where a widow would help him. The widow had very little. But she offered him all she had – a handful of flour in a jar and a little oil.

Elijah told the widow to go and make a small loaf of bread.

"God has told me that the jar of flour will never be empty and the jug of oil will never run dry until the day the rains come again!" said Elijah.

This is exactly what happened. So the Lord provided again for all Elijah's needs.

1 Kings 17, verses 7 to 16

Prayer:

Dear God, thank you for people who help me. Please show me how I can help those around me.

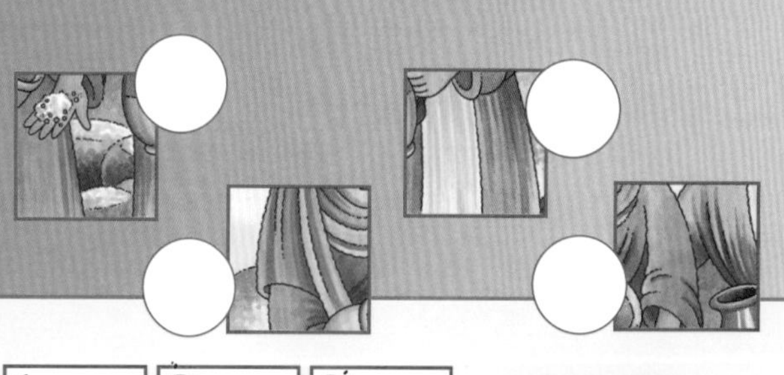

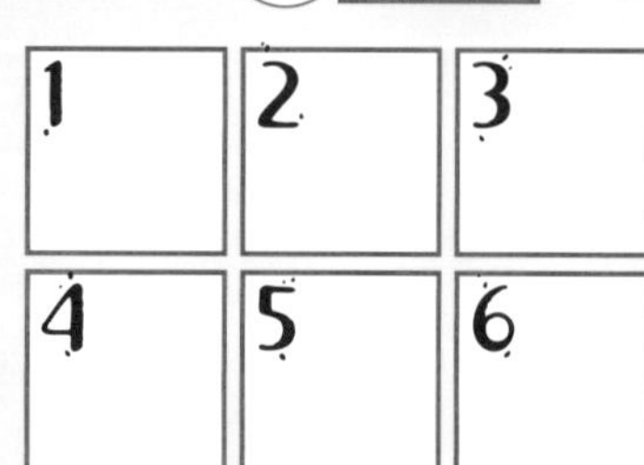

Activity:

To re-create this picture the squares have to be put in the correct place. Can you put the correct position number in each circle?

1	2	3
4	5	6
7	8	9

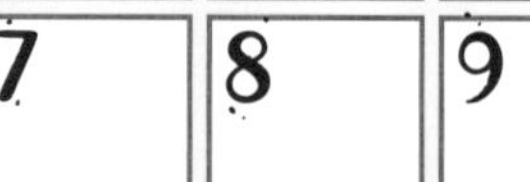

✎ Activity:

Can you draw a line from each fragment to the place on the big picture where the fragment comes from?

Something to think about:

If we trust God, he will provide us with all the things we need.

Elijah brings a boy back to life

One day, the son of the widow became very ill. He got worse and worse. Then he stopped breathing.

His mother was frantic.

"Elijah!" she shouted. "How could you let this happen to me?"

Elijah took the little boy in his arms and carried him upstairs. He laid him down on the bed and cried out to God three times:

"Lord God, let this boy's life come back to him!"

God listened to Elijah. He brought the little boy back to life.

Elijah took the boy back to his mother. She was overjoyed! She knew that Elijah was a special man of God.

1 Kings 17, verses 17 to 24

Activity:

Six of these circular details are taken from the big picture. Put a checkmark under the ones that come from the big picture and an X under the ones that don't.

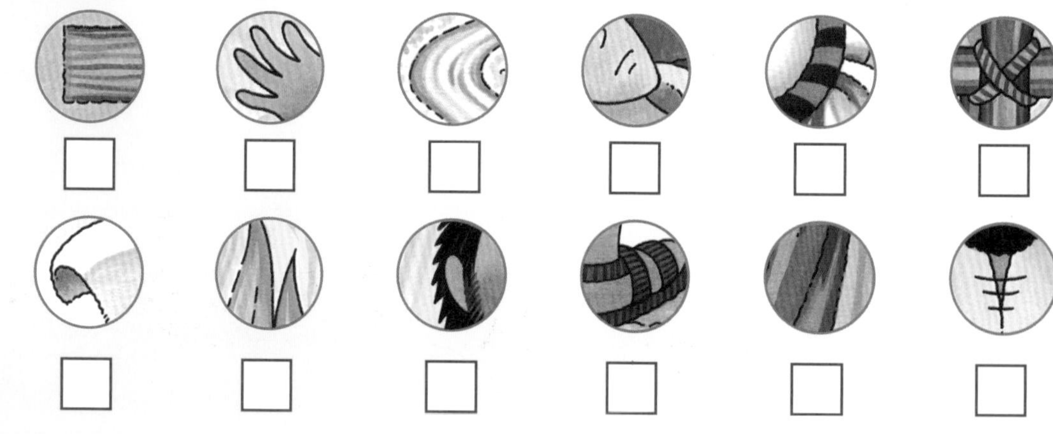

Something to think about:

God can do amazing things! He brought the little boy back to life.

Prayer:

Dear God, please help the people I know who are ill. Please look after...

Elijah returns to Ahab

After more than three years of drought and famine in the land, God told Elijah to return to Ahab. This was a dangerous thing to do, as Ahab was still trying to kill God's prophets.

Elijah spoke boldly to Ahab.

"You have turned away from God and worshipped Baal instead," he said.

Elijah knew that Ahab and his wife had been worshipping other gods. He also knew that only his God, the God of Israel, was real and able to answer prayer. He told Ahab that he must change his ways and come back to the one true God.

1 Kings 18, verses 1 to 18

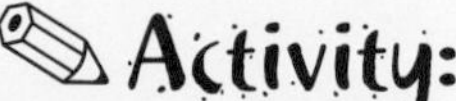

Activity:

Can you complete the big picture by coloring it in?
Choose your own colors or use this small picture as a guide.

Activity:

Unscramble the letters to find a word that describes Elijah.

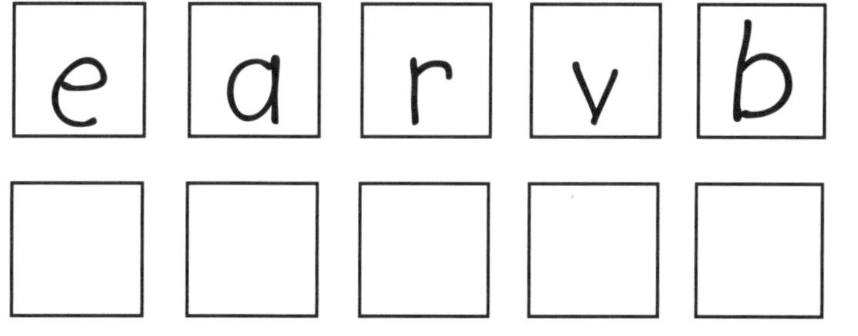

Something to think about:

God can help us in difficult situations, even when we may be afraid.

Prayer:

Dear God, please help me to be brave when I...

A challenge for the true God

"Bring all the prophets of Baal to Mount Carmel," said Elijah. "We will have a contest to see who is the true God. Then you will know whom to worship."

Elijah explained what the contest would be:

"Get two bulls. The prophets of Baal can have one and put it on their altar. I will put the other bull on the altar of the Lord. Then the prophets of Baal can call upon him to send fire to burn up their offering. I will call on God to do the same. Whoever answers with fire is the true God."

1 Kings 18, verses 19 to 25

Prayer:
Help me to know you are real, dear God, and expect you to act in my life.

Something to think about:

Ask God to help and he will prove that he is real.

Activity:

Can you spot the ten differences in the two pictures? Mark the box and draw a line from it to where the change is.

1 ☐
2 ☐
3 ☐
4 ☐
5 ☐
6 ☐
7 ☐
8 ☐
9 ☐
10 ☐

The contest on the mountain

Q	E	N	Y	I	E	S	S	Y
W	R	M	M	O	D	Y	C	I
A	E	B	A	A	L	B	S	J
T	I	R	Z	C	F	D	E	H
E	T	A	Z	W	I	E	R	Y
R	L	G	E	I	R	R	V	M
T	R	D	F	J	E	E	A	P
M	I	P	S	D	R	I	N	Z
A	D	R	I	Y	S	T	T	U
W	L	O	R	D	Y	L	S	E
S	T	P	Y	N	B	U	L	L
S	S	H	M	P	M	J	R	S
Y	C	E	L	I	J	A	H	I
A	L	T	A	R	W	R	W	F
D	E	S	U	R	O	S	A	Y

Activity:

Can you find all of the following words in the word box above?

BAAL FIRE PROPHETS ELIJAH ALTAR JARS SERVANTS BULL WATER LORD

The prophets of Baal called to Baal from morning till noon, but there was no fire.

"Shout louder!" said Elijah. "Perhaps he is asleep!"

All day long, the prophets shouted loudly to Baal. But no fire came.

Then Elijah prepared the altar of the Lord. He put the bull on it.

"Now fill four large jars with water and pour it on top," said Elijah to the servants. "Do this three times!"

Soon the altar was soaked with water. How could it possibly burn now?

Elijah stepped forward and prayed:

"Oh Lord God, please answer me. Show these people that you are the real God. Help them to know you and worship you again."

1 Kings 18, verses 26 to 37

Something to think about:

God answers when we call to him.

Prayer:

Dear God, I need you to help me when I am...

The people worship God

Suddenly, God sent fire to burn up the bull on the altar and all the water around it. Everyone was amazed.

They threw themselves to the ground, shouting, "The Lord is God!"

"Seize the prophets of Baal!" shouted Elijah.

They were taken away and killed.

"Go and eat and drink, Ahab!" said Elijah to the king. "There is the sound of heavy rain."

A small rain cloud, the size of a man's fist, appeared in the sky. It became larger and larger, and soon the rains fell again. God had sent fire and rain. He had shown that he was the true God.

1 Kings 18, verses 38 to 46

Something to think about:

God is faithful. He will not let us down when we put our trust in him.

Prayer:

Dear God, thank you for hearing me when I talk to you.

Activity:

Can you tell who these people are?

Which of them do you think worshipped the true God?

Elijah flees to Sinai

When Ahab's wife, Jezebel, heard that all the prophets of Baal had been killed, she sent a message to Elijah. She wanted him dead.

Elijah was frightened and ran away.

In the desert, Elijah sat down under a broom tree and prayed to God:

"Lord, I've had enough of all this. I can't go on."

Elijah fell asleep under the tree.

Suddenly an angel tapped him on the arm and said, "Get up and eat!"

Elijah looked and saw some freshly baked bread and a jar of water. He ate and drank and then went back to sleep.

The angel woke him up again and told him to eat and drink some more. Elijah did as he was told and felt much stronger.

He travelled on for forty days until he reached Sinai, the mountain of God, where he went into a cave for the night.

1 Kings 19, verses 1 to 8

Something to think about:

Can you remember another time when God provided food for Elijah?

Activity:

What will you discover when you join all the dots? You can finish the picture and color it in.

Prayer:

Dear God, help me not to give up easily when things seem difficult.

The Lord appears to Elijah

Elijah heard God's voice as he hid in the cave: "What are you doing, Elijah?"

Elijah answered, "I am the only one left who worships you. They are trying to kill me now too."

God said, "Go and stand on the mountain, for the Lord is soon going to pass by."

A mighty wind blew against the mountain so hard that rocks shattered. But the Lord was not in the wind.

There was a mighty earthquake. But the Lord was not in the earthquake.

There was a great fire. But the Lord was not in the fire.

Then there was a gentle whisper. When Elijah heard it, he hid his face in his cloak and stood at the mouth of the cave. God spoke to Elijah and told him to make Jehu king of Israel, and to make Elisha the next prophet.

Activity:

Which path leads to the top of the mountain?

a

b

c

Prayer:

Dear God, you spoke to Elijah in a gentle whisper. Help me to know your voice.

Something to think about:

Even though he is very powerful, God spoke to Elijah in a gentle whisper.

The chariot of fire

Elijah chose Elisha to be the next prophet, just as God told him. Elisha stayed with Elijah and learned from him.

At the end of Elijah's life, Elijah and Elisha travelled together. They went from place to place, and Elisha would not let Elijah go on without him.

"Let me serve God after you," asked Elisha. "Let me have God's power to help people as you have done."

"Only God can give you this power," said Elijah. "If you see me leave you, then your prayer will be answered."

Suddenly a chariot of fire pulled by horses of fire appeared. Elijah was taken up to heaven in a whirlwind.

Elisha watched as Elijah went from his sight.

Then he picked up Elijah's cloak and struck the waters of the River Jordan with it – and the water parted so he could walk across. God had answered his prayer.

2 Kings 2, verses 1 to 14

Prayer:

Dear God, thank you for my friends and teachers. Help me to follow their example and be someone others can follow.

Something to think about:

Elisha learned how to serve God by following Elijah's example right to the end of Elijah's life.

Activity:

Can you draw a line between each pair of people or things that have a special connection?

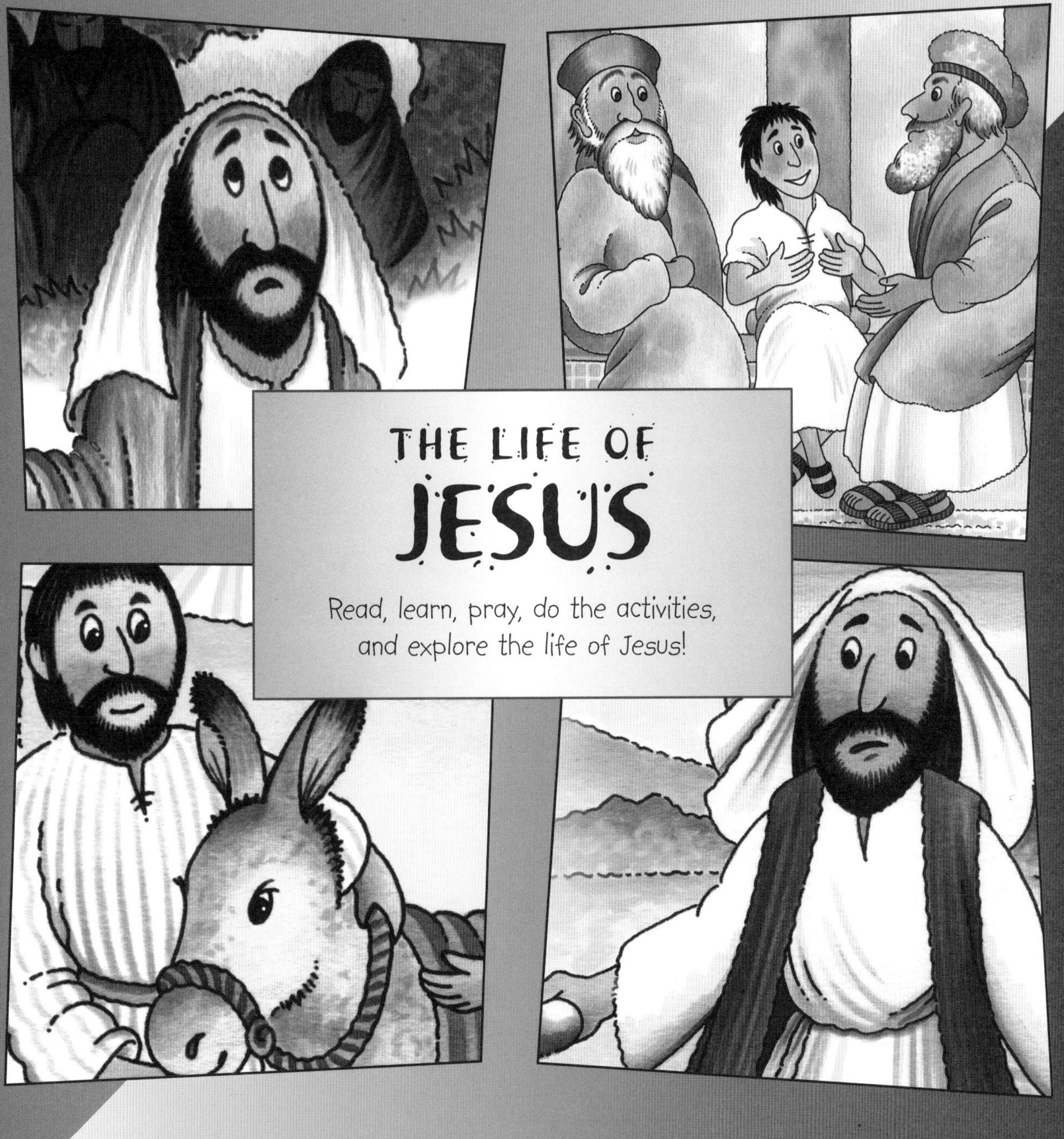
THE LIFE OF
JESUS
Read, learn, pray, do the activities,
and explore the life of Jesus!

Jesus is born

An angel brought good news to Mary: "You will have a baby! Call him Jesus. He will be God's son!"

Mary and her husband Joseph had to travel a very long way to Bethlehem. There was nowhere for them to stay: all the inns in the town were full. So they settled down with the animals in a warm room behind the inn. Jesus – God's own son – was born. Mary wrapped him up warmly and placed him in a manger.

That night, shepherds on the hills near Bethlehem had a great surprise. An angel appeared, saying, "Don't be afraid! I bring good news for you and all the world. Today in Bethlehem your Savior is born. Go and find him. He is wrapped in cloths and lying in a manger."

The shepherds hurried to find the baby. They praised God for what they had seen.

Wise men came from the east, looking for a new King. They brought gifts of gold, frankincense and myrrh to Jesus and worshipped him.

Luke 2, verses 4 to 20;
Matthew 2, verses 1 to 12

Something to think about:

All new babies are special, but what was so special about Jesus?

Activity:

These animals were born in a stable too. Can you complete the pictures?

Activity:

Can you find four mistakes in this picture of Mary and Joseph?

Prayer:

Dear God, thank you for sending Jesus to be born as a baby. Help me to remember him all year round, not just at Christmas.

Where is Jesus?

When Jesus was twelve years old, he went to Jerusalem with Mary and Joseph for the Passover feast. Many people from his home town went together. It was a great celebration.

When it was time to go home, Jesus stayed behind in Jerusalem. But Mary and Joseph did not notice. They thought he was playing with his friends. Mary began to get very worried, and they turned back to Jerusalem to look for Jesus.

Three days later, they found Jesus. He was in the temple courts, speaking to a group of teachers. Everyone was amazed at the things Jesus said. He seemed to know so much about God.

"My son!" said Mary. "Don't you know how worried we have been?"

"Mother," said Jesus, "didn't you know I would be here in my Father's house?"

But Mary and Joseph did not understand what he meant.

Luke 2, verses 41 to 52

Activity:

Cross out the birds which were not sacrificed in the temple:

flamingos pigeons robins

Something to think about:

Why did Jesus call the temple "my Father's house"?

Prayer:

Dear God, help me to learn more about you.

Activity:

Can you color in this picture of Mary and Joseph?

Activity:

Can you find the matching pair of candle stands?

Jesus is baptized

John the Baptist told people to be prepared for the coming of God's Kingdom.

"Say sorry to God for all the wrong things you have done, and be baptized!" he said.

Prayer:

Dear God, I am sorry for the wrong things I have done, especially... Thank you that you forgive me when I am sorry.

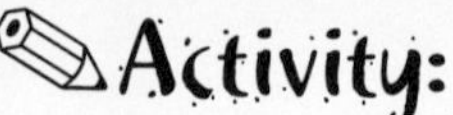

Activity:

Color in the dotted pieces of this picture and see what you can find.

John baptized them in the River Jordan as a sign of God washing their sins away.

When Jesus was about thirty years old, he came to see John on the bank of the river.

"I want you to baptize me in the river," said Jesus.

John was very surprised. He knew that Jesus had done nothing wrong, so he didn't need to be baptized. But Jesus asked him again, and John baptized him.

When Jesus came out of the river, heaven opened and he saw a dove, and a voice spoke: "This is my dear son, with whom I am pleased."

It was God's voice speaking.

Matthew 3, verses 13 to 17

Something to think about:

God loves to forgive us when we say sorry.

Activity:

Match the picture details and write their identification letters in the correct boxes.

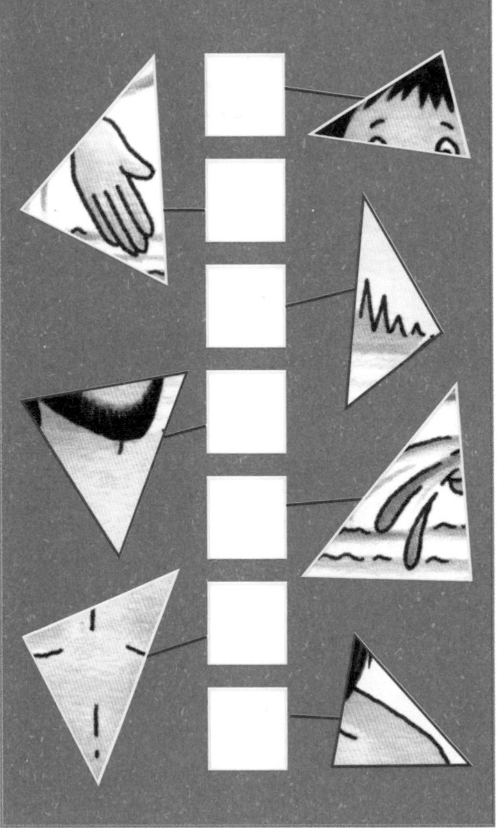

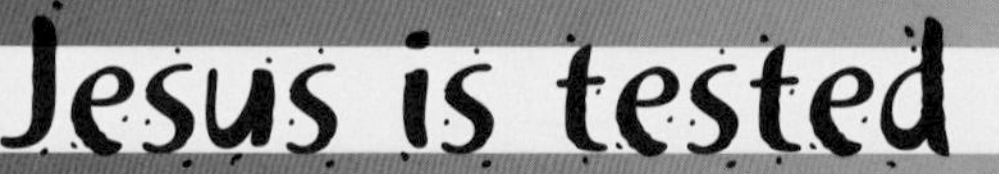

Jesus is tested

Something to think about:

Jesus used words from the Bible when he was tested. Do you know any words from the Bible by heart?

After Jesus was baptized, he was led by God into the desert and ate nothing for forty days and nights. The devil came and tested Jesus.

First the devil told Jesus to turn stones into bread.

But Jesus replied with words from Scripture, saying, "People cannot live on bread alone but need every word that God has spoken."

Then the devil took Jesus to the top of the temple and told him to throw himself off so that the angels would catch him.

But Jesus replied: "It is written, 'Do not put God to the test.' "

Lastly the devil took Jesus to a high mountain and promised to give Jesus all the kingdoms of the earth, if he would only bow down and worship him. But Jesus did not give in.

"It is written, 'Worship the Lord your God and serve him alone,' " he said. Then the devil went away. Angels came to be with Jesus.

Matthew 4, verses 1 to 11

Activity:

Which words in the list below describe Jesus? Underline them in red. Which words describe the devil? Underline them in black.

wicked	liar
proud	humble
truthful	good
cunning	hungry
loving	selfish

Prayer:

Dear God, please help me to talk to you when I am being tested or in a difficult situation.

Jesus the King

Jesus and his friends were on their way to Jerusalem for the Passover festival.

Jesus sent two of his friends on ahead, saying, "Go to the village over there and find a young donkey. Bring it to me. Say that your master needs it."

The two friends went and got the donkey, put their cloaks over the donkey's back, and Jesus sat on it.

Jesus rode into the great city of Jerusalem. Huge

Something to think about:

Jesus was a king, but he rode into Jerusalem on a donkey. Why?

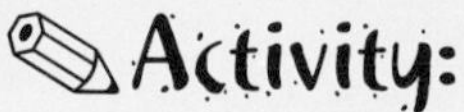

Activity:

Can you find the ten differences in the picture opposite?

crowds came to greet him, spreading their cloaks on the road and waving palm branches. They greeted him as their King.

"Hosanna!" they shouted. "Blessed is he who comes in the name of the Lord!"

Some teachers from the temple were angry with Jesus. They wanted to get rid of him. But Jesus entered Jerusalem and went to the temple.

Mark 11, verses 1 to 11

Prayer:

Dear God, thank you for sending Jesus to be the King of Kings.

The last supper

Prayer:

Dear God, help me to remember all that Jesus did for us.

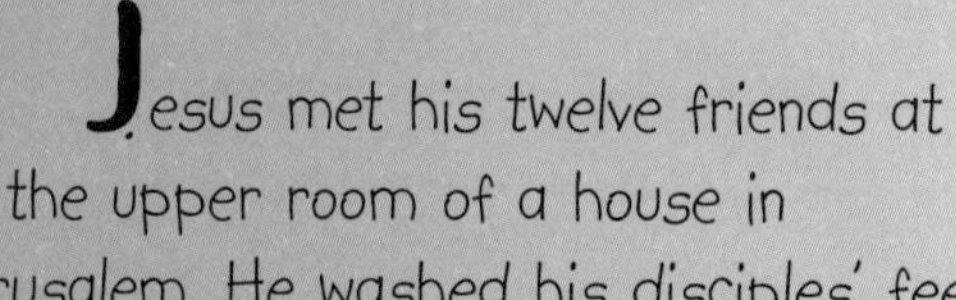

Jesus met his twelve friends at the upper room of a house in Jerusalem. He washed his disciples' feet, then reclined at the table with his friends, ready to eat the Passover meal.

Jesus looked at his friends gathered around him and said, "One of you is going to hand me over to be killed."

It would be Judas Iscariot.

Jesus took some bread, broke it and gave it to his friends. "Eat this and remember me," said Jesus. "This is my body."

Then he took the cup of wine, thanked God for it, and handed it round. "Drink this and remember me," said Jesus. "This is my blood, given for many."

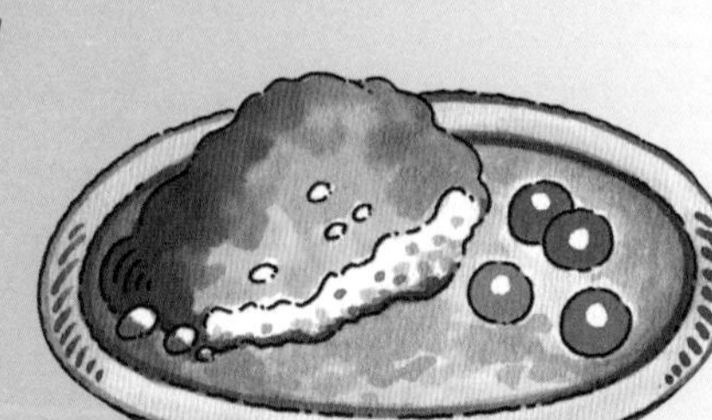

They sang a song to God, then went to the Mount of Olives to pray.

Mark 14, verses 12 to 26

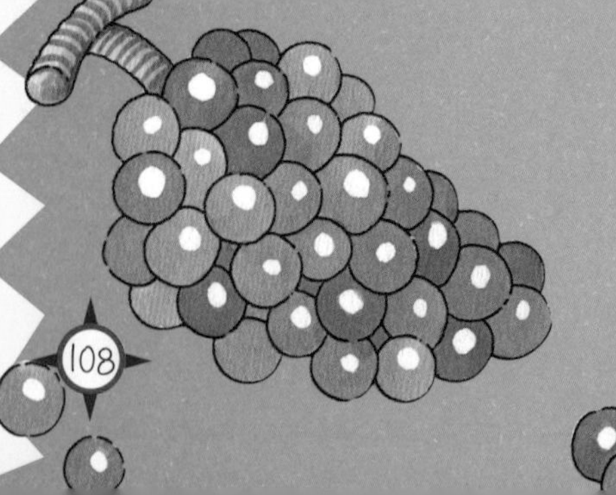

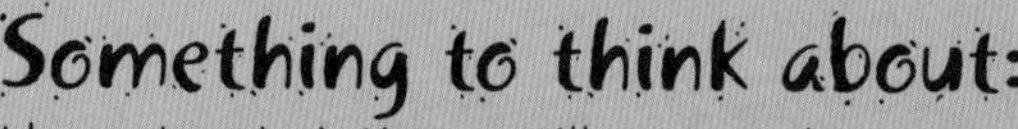

Something to think about:

How do Christians still remember Jesus giving the bread and wine?

Activity:

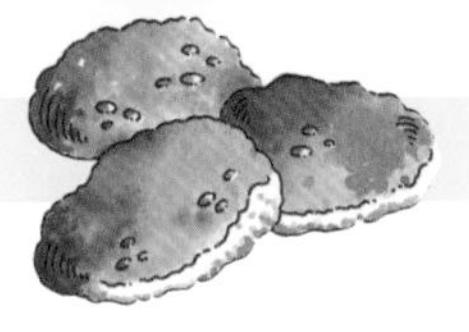

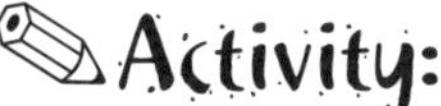

Can you draw some cups and plates on the table?

Activity:

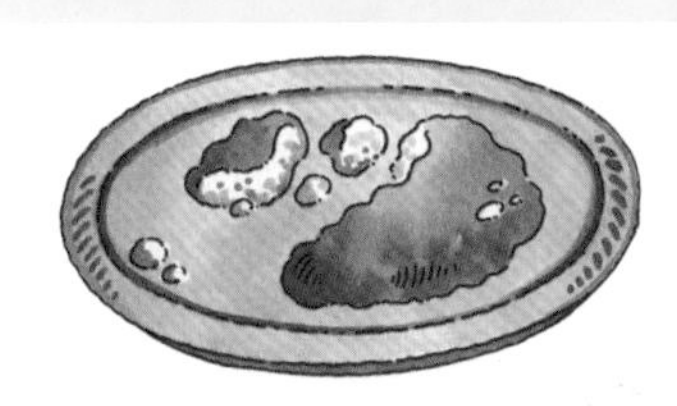

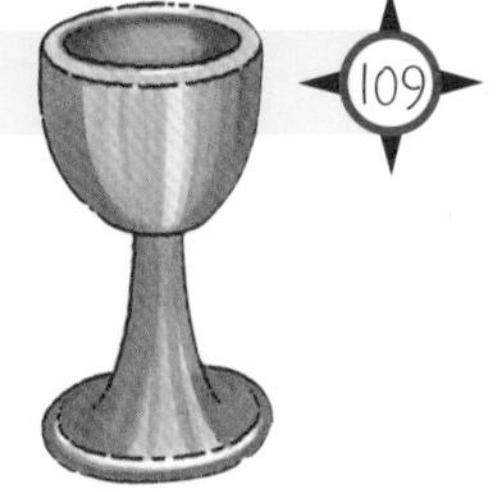

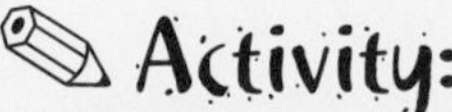

Locate each person at the table. Connect them with a line. Which one is not at the table?

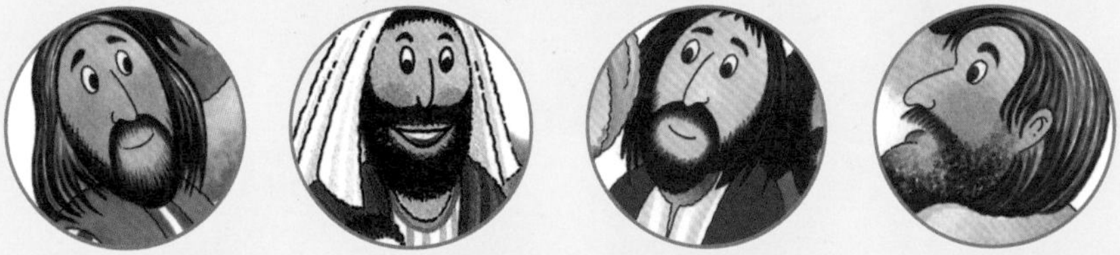

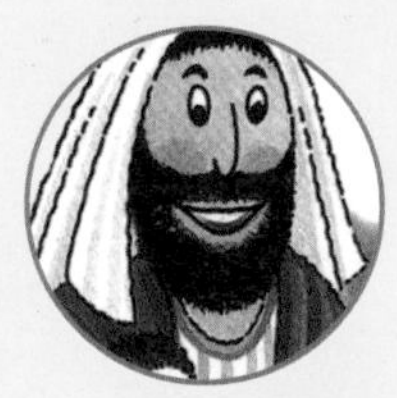

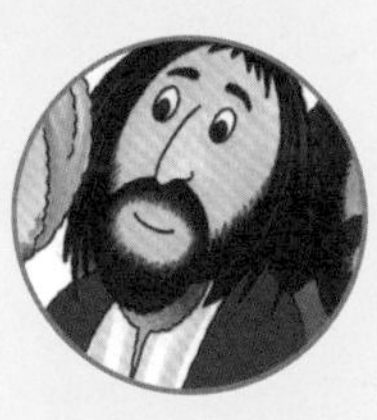

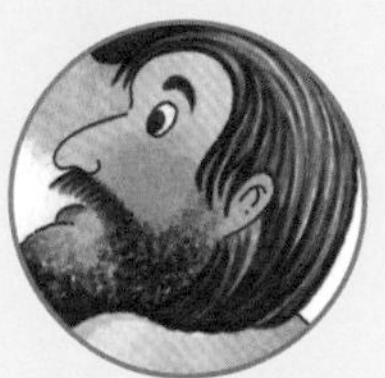

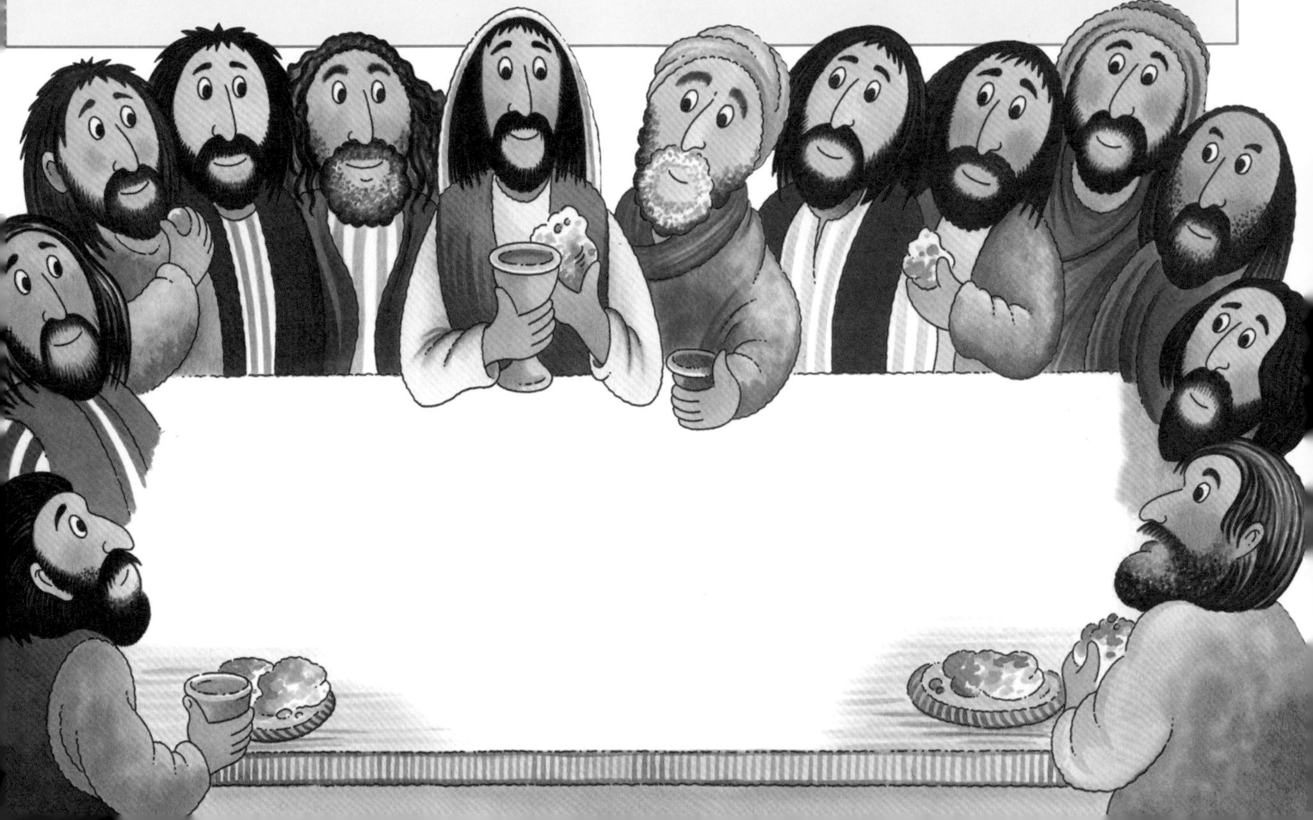

Jesus in the garden

On the Mount of Olives was a garden called Gethsemane. Here Jesus knelt down to pray to God. He knew that the time was coming for him to be taken away from his friends. Tears ran down his face as he prayed to God, his Father in heaven.

Jesus asked his friends to pray with him. But they kept falling asleep.

"Why are you sleeping?" he asked them. "Watch and pray with me."

Suddenly a crowd came towards them, and Judas Iscariot was with them. Soldiers and chief priests followed closely behind. Judas came near to Jesus to kiss him. This showed the soldiers where Jesus was.

Jesus was arrested and taken away to see the High Priest.

Mark 14, verses 32 to 50

Activity:

Can you find the one matching pair of butterflies? Put a circle around them.

Prayer:

Dear God, please help me to watch and pray for the people around me and the things I see.

Activity:

Make a pattern on the butterfly wings and color it in to make a beautiful butterfly for the garden.

Something to think about:

If you had been with Jesus, would you have prayed with him or fallen asleep?

Jesus on trial

Jesus was brought before Pilate, the Roman governor.

"What has this man done wrong?" Pilate asked the crowd.

"He is causing trouble all over the country," said the chief priests. "He says he is a king."

"Are you the King of the Jews?" asked Pilate.

"Yes, it is as you say," said Jesus.

"What shall I do with Jesus?" Pilate asked the crowd.

"Put him on a cross to die!" the people shouted.

Pilate did not think Jesus had done anything wrong, but he wanted to please the crowd. So he handed Jesus over to the soldiers to be killed. His soldiers put a purple robe on Jesus and a crown of thorns on his head.

Mark 15, verses 1 to 17

Something to think about:

Pilate tried to please the crowd, rather than doing what he thought was the fair thing to do. Do you ever listen to what people think rather than doing what's right?

Prayer:

Dear God, I am sorry for times when I have not been fair to other people.

Activity:

Can you answer all these questions about Jesus?

How many presents did the wise men bring for baby Jesus? (See page 98)	
How many palm trees are shown on page 99?	
How old was Jesus when his parents lost him in the temple? (See page 100)	
How many special friends did Jesus have? (See page 109 and count them)	
How many friends was Jesus was betrayed by? (See page 110)	
How many things did the soldiers give Jesus to wear? (the answer is on this page)	
Add up all the answers above to find out how old Jesus was when he died.	

Jesus dies on a cross

Jesus was taken by the soldiers to a place called Golgotha. There he was nailed to a cross. Above his head was a sign which said "The King of the Jews."

Jesus' mother, Mary, stood close by and watched. Darkness covered the land. At the ninth hour, Jesus cried out in a loud voice to God, then breathed his last breath. Jesus died.

Jesus' body was taken down from the cross. It was wrapped in cloths and carefully placed in a tomb belonging to Joseph of Arimathea. A very heavy round stone was rolled across the doorway of the tomb.

Jesus' friends thought they would never see him again. They went home and wept.

Mark 15, verses 20 to 47

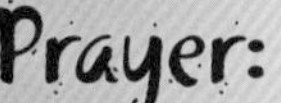

Prayer:

Dear God, help me to understand more about what Jesus did for us.

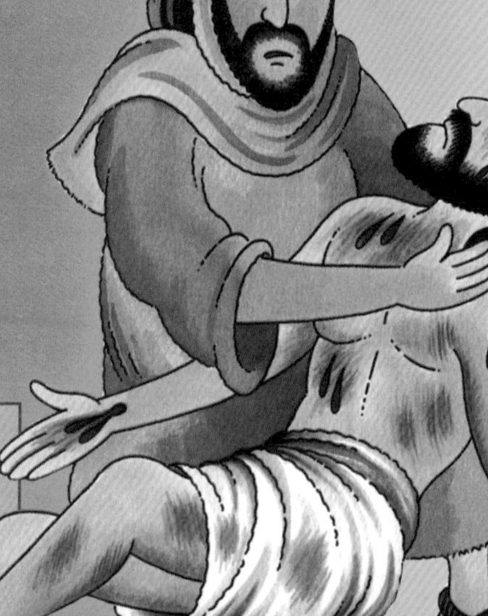

Something to think about:

Have you ever wondered why Jesus had to die on a cross?

Activity:

Can you find these words?

- ☐ JESUS
- ☐ GOLGOTHA
- ☐ MARY
- ☐ JOSEPH
- ☐ TOMB
- ☐ DARK

Q	M	I	N	S	F	P	D
J	G	I	Y	J	S	P	A
O	O	G	U	E	S	Y	R
S	L	C	R	A	L	S	K
E	G	J	E	S	U	S	A
P	O	O	T	O	M	B	C
H	T	S	D	U	A	F	E
T	H	E	R	S	R	I	S
H	A	P	E	Z	Y	S	U
O	T	H	S	I	A	H	R

Activity:

Darkness covered the land before Jesus died.

Can you tell what these silhouettes are?

Jesus is alive!

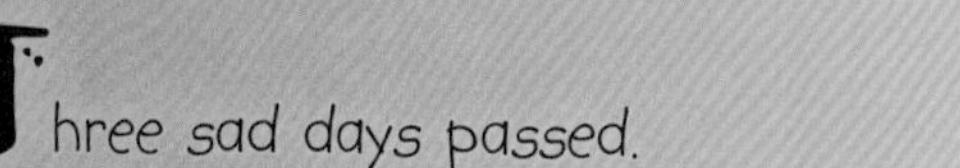

Three sad days passed.

Early on Sunday morning, some of the women went to his tomb with special spices. What a shock they had when they got there! The large stone which blocked the entrance to the tomb had been rolled away! The tomb was empty!

Jesus' body had gone. All that was left were the strips of cloth which Jesus' body had been wrapped in.

Suddenly two men in bright shining clothes appeared.

"Don't look for Jesus here," they said. "He is alive!"

The women ran home at once and told Jesus' friends.

Over the next few days, Jesus appeared to all his disciples. At first, some were not sure it was Jesus. Some did not believe until they saw the wounds in Jesus' hands. But soon everyone knew – Jesus really was alive!

Luke 24, verses 1 to 43

Activity:

Can you help Mary find the right way to the tomb?

Prayer:

Dear God, thank you for making Jesus come alive again so that we can know him too!

Something to think about:

Would you have believed that Jesus was alive again?

Jesus returns to heaven

Jesus saw his friends many times over the next few days.

"Don't leave Jerusalem," he told his disciples, "but wait for the gift which God has promised to give you – the Holy Spirit. When he comes, you will be able to tell the whole world about me!"

After forty days, Jesus was taken up to heaven. He was hidden from sight by a cloud.

As the disciples were looking at the sky, two men in white clothes stood beside them.

"Why are you looking at the sky?" they asked the disciples. "Jesus will return one day in the same way as you saw him go."

Acts 1, verses 1 to 11

Activity:
On what page can you find a blue dragonfly? ☐

Something to think about:
Who do you think the men in white clothes were?

Activity:

Find and mark the odd one out.

Activity:

Find and circle three of a kind.

Prayer:

Dear God, thank you that Jesus will come back again one day. Help me to be ready for him.

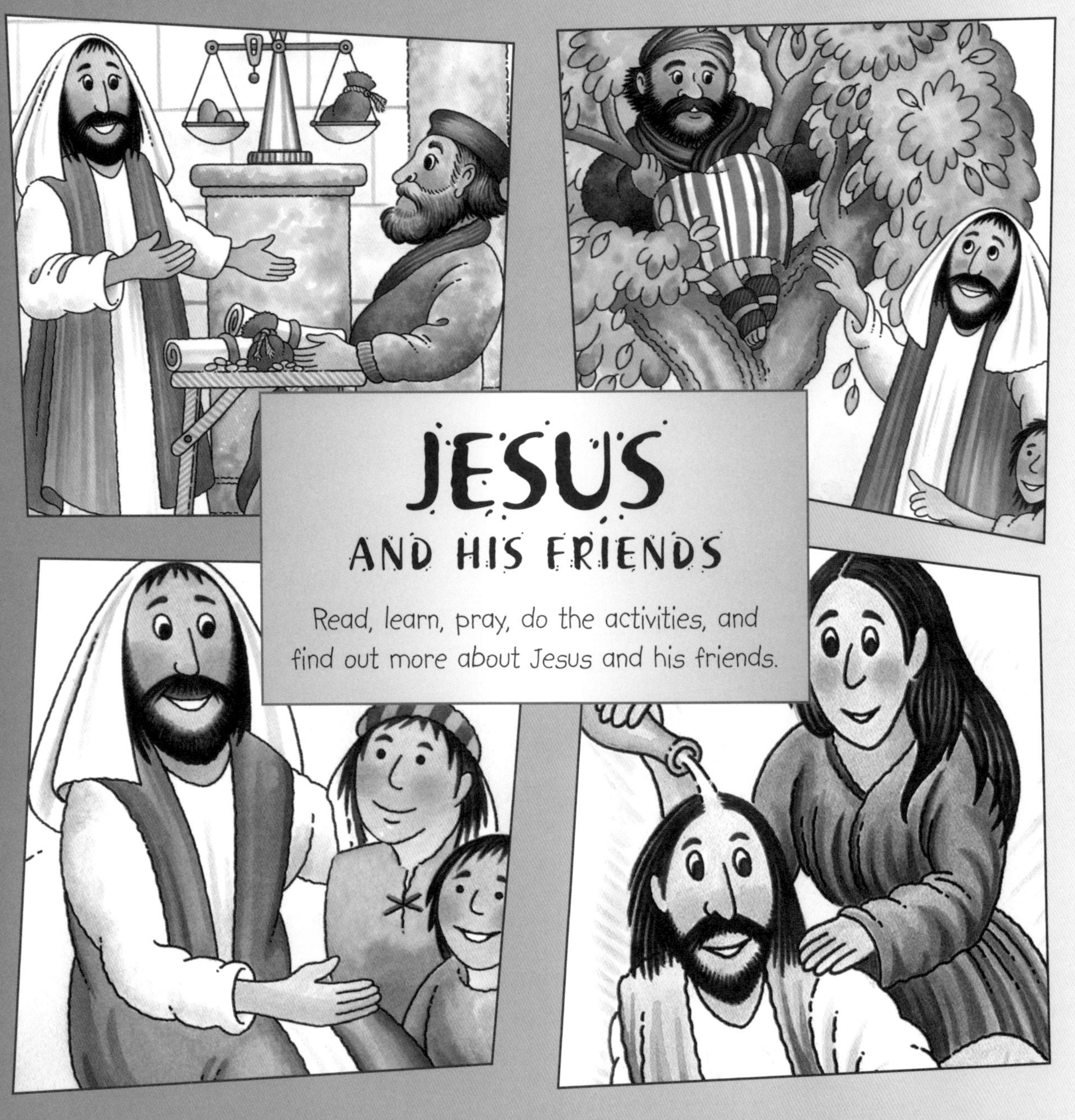

JESUS AND HIS FRIENDS

Read, learn, pray, do the activities, and find out more about Jesus and his friends.

Jesus chooses his first disciples

One day Jesus was speaking to crowds of people on the shore of Lake Galilee.

Jesus stepped into a boat belonging to Simon and spoke from the boat.

When he had finished speaking, Jesus asked Simon to row the boat out into the deeper water and let down the nets.

"We've worked hard all night," said Simon, "and haven't caught a single sardine. But if you tell me, I'll do it."

So off they went – and their nets were filled to overflowing with fish!

Simon was amazed. He knew there was something very special about Jesus. James and John, Simon's partners, couldn't believe their eyes either.

"Don't be afraid," said Jesus. "Follow me. I will make you fishers of people."

So the fishermen left their nets and followed Jesus.

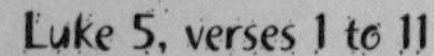
Luke 5, verses 1 to 11

Something to think about:

Jesus asked the fishermen to follow him and they did so.

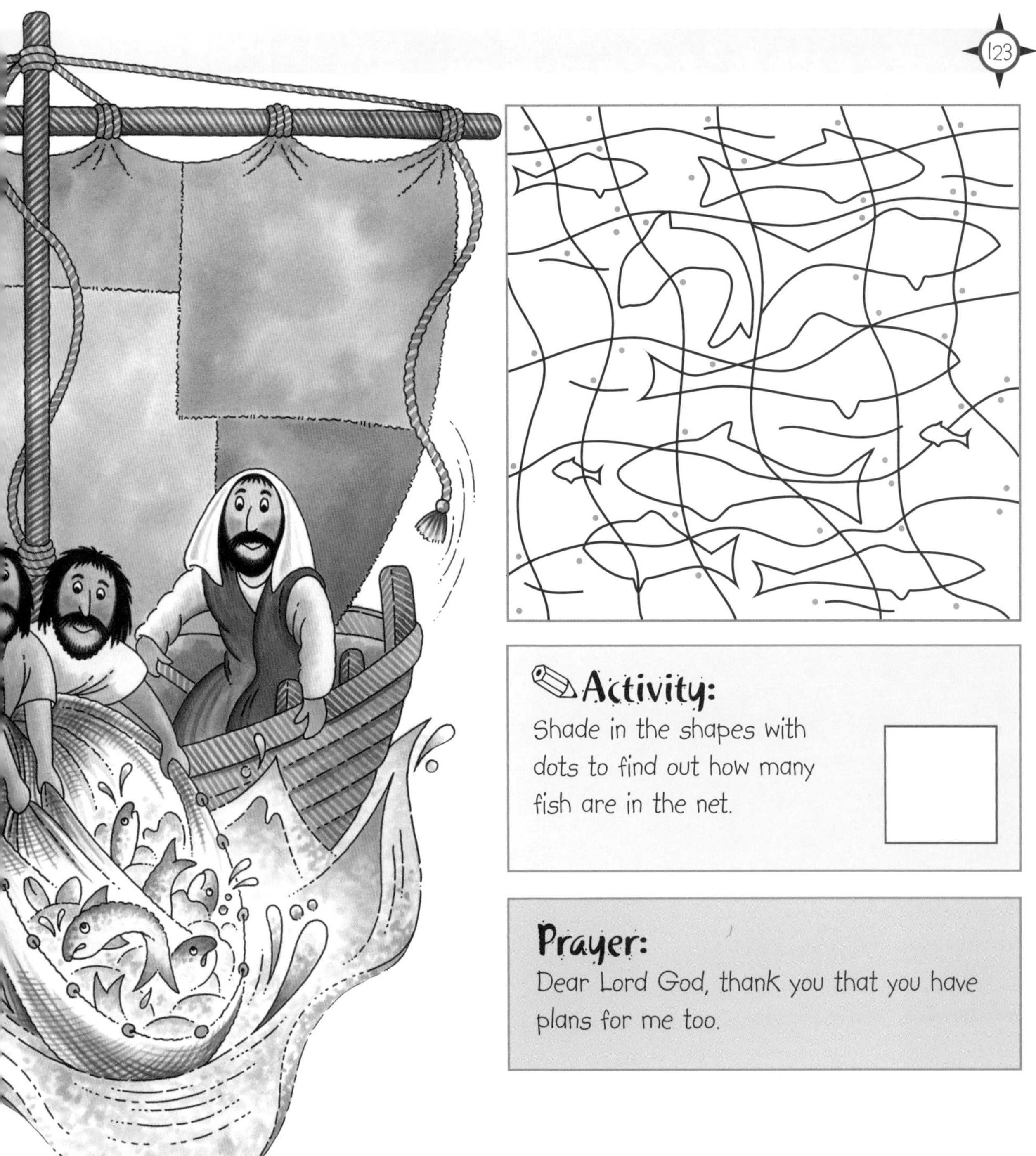

Activity:

Shade in the shapes with dots to find out how many fish are in the net.

Prayer:

Dear Lord God, thank you that you have plans for me too.

Jesus chooses a tax collector

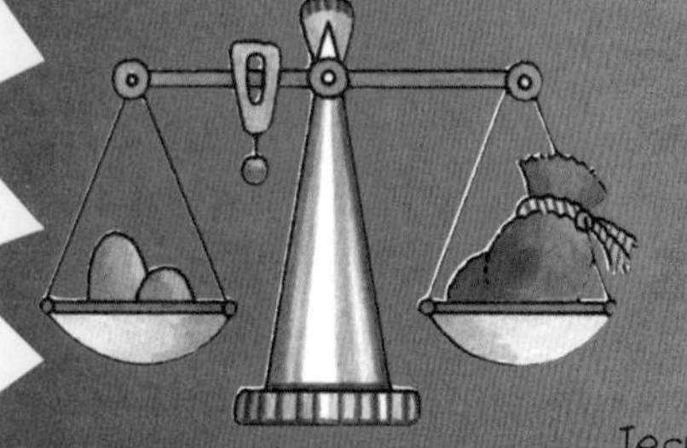

Jesus saw a tax collector called Matthew sitting at the place where Jews paid taxes to the Romans. Everyone hated the tax collectors.

Jesus spoke to Matthew. "Come and follow me!" he said.

At once Matthew left everything and went away with Jesus.

He held a big meal at his home for Jesus. He invited other tax collectors and guests.

Some teachers of the Law muttered to each other. Then they spoke to Jesus' disciples.

"Why do you eat and drink with those people?" they asked.

Jesus heard them and answered, "I came to invite them to know God." he said. "They need to know how much God loves them, just like everyone else."

Matthew 9, verses 9 to 13

Something to think about:

Jesus especially welcomed people who were hated by other people.

Activity:

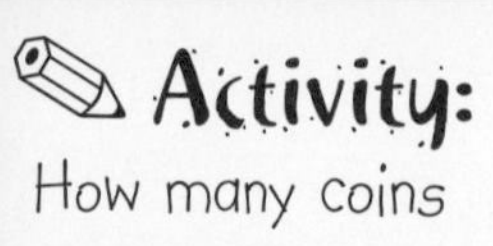

How many coins are there?

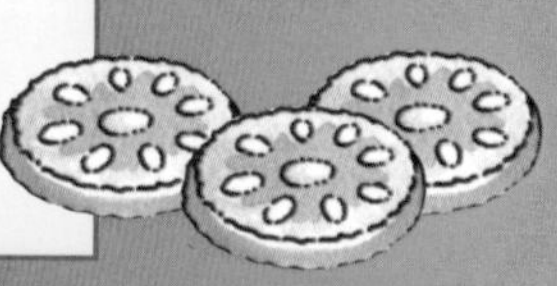

+

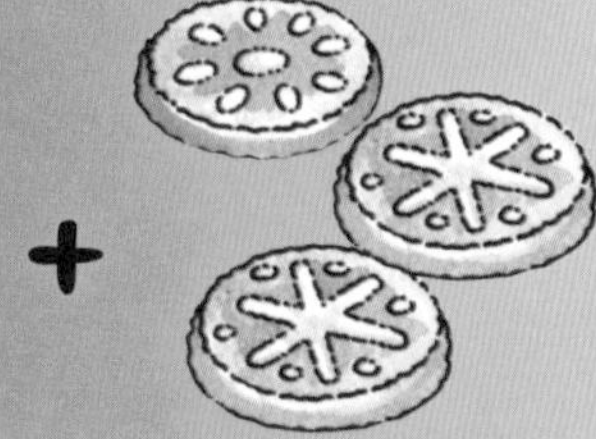

=

Prayer:

Dear God, help me to accept and love other people as Jesus did.

Activity:

Can you design your own coin? Draw a face, picture or pattern in the blank coin above.

+ =

+ =

Jesus blesses the children

People loved to bring their children to Jesus for him to bless. Jesus welcomed them with open arms.

But Jesus' friends were not very happy about it.

"Don't bother him with the children," they said to the mothers and fathers who brought their children to Jesus. "Jesus is too busy."

Jesus overheard them. Jesus was never too busy for children.

"Let the children come to me," he said. "Don't try to stop them. My Kingdom belongs to people who are like these children. You will never enter God's Kingdom if you don't enter it like a child."

Luke 18, verses 15 to 17

Something to think about:

What did Jesus mean about God's Kingdom belonging to children?

Prayer:

Dear God, thank you that you love me and always have time for me.

Activity:

Can you help this child to find his way through the maze to Jesus?

Zacchaeus

Jesus was walking through Jericho. A man lived there called Zacchaeus. He was a very rich man and was in charge of collecting taxes in the area.

Zacchaeus was a very short man. He heard that Jesus was coming, but he wasn't tall enough to see over the heads of the crowd. So he climbed a tree to see Jesus.

Jesus called to him in the tree: "Zacchaeus, come down! I want to come to your house today."

Zacchaeus was very pleased to welcome Jesus to his house. But other people started complaining.

"Zacchaeus is a *bad* man! Why does Jesus want to eat with him?" they asked.

Zacchaeus later told the crowds of people that he was going to change for the *better*:

"I want to give half of all I own to the poor. If I have cheated anyone, I will pay them *back* four times as much."

Luke 19, verses 1 to 10

Something to think about:

Zacchaeus wanted to change when he met Jesus. He became a generous man.

Prayer:

Dear God, thank you that you are interested in everyone, even when other people have no time for them.

Activity:

Can you find ten differences between the two pictures?

A gift for Jesus

Something to think about:

The woman gave Jesus a very special gift. What would you give to Jesus?

Prayer:

Dear God, thank you for all that Jesus has given me. Help me to know what I can do today to please him.

While Jesus was in Bethany he had dinner with a man named Simon.

A woman came into the room with a very expensive bottle of perfume. She poured it on Jesus' head while he sat at the table. The smell of the perfume wafted through the whole house.

"Why waste all that money on that perfume?" someone muttered. "It could have been sold for a high price, and the money could have been given to the poor!"

Jesus answered, "Leave her alone! She has done a very special thing. You will always have the poor, but you won't always have me."

Jesus knew that he was soon going to die.

Matthew 26, verses 6 to 13

Activity:

Can you find three identical pairs of presents? Connect each pair with a line.

Activity:
Can you color the gift box below to look like the one above?
Now design and color your own wrapping for the gift below.

Jesus brings Lazarus back to life

Jesus had a good friend called Lazarus, who lived in a town many miles away. Jesus heard that Lazarus was ill. But by the time Jesus reached the town, Lazarus was dead.

Jesus wept. He had loved his friend. He went to the tomb where Lazarus' body had been put. It had been there for four days already. A large stone was rolled across the tomb.

Jesus told some men to roll the stone aside. He prayed aloud to God. "Thank you, Father, that you hear my prayers."

Then Jesus shouted, "Come out, Lazarus!"

Lazarus walked out into the daylight, still covered in his grave clothes, with a cloth over his face, but very much alive!

Many people watching now knew that Jesus had been sent from God. They began to see that they could trust him to help them.

John 11, verses 1 to 45

Something to think about:

Jesus understands about the things that make us sad. He cried when he found that his friend had died.

Prayer:

Dear God, thank you that Jesus showed us your amazing power, even to bring the dead back to life.

Activity:

Can you find the eight picture fragments in the big picture?

Write the number of each fragment in the boxes provided.

Jesus washes his friends' feet

Jesus met his twelve friends in the upper room of a house in Jerusalem. It was time for the Passover feast.

c

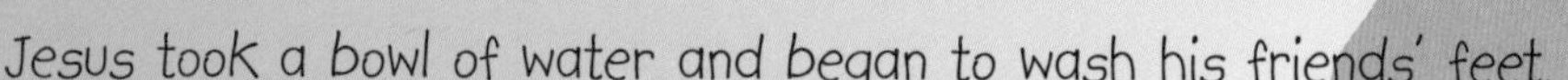

Jesus took a bowl of water and began to wash his friends' feet.

a

"Don't wash my feet!" said Peter. "You're our master, not our servant!"

"Unless I wash you, you don't belong to me," said Jesus.

Peter was astonished but his answer was quick:

"Then wash my hands and head as well!"

But Jesus said that only his feet needed washing. Peter let Jesus wash them.

"Now that I have washed your feet," said Jesus, "you must also wash each other's feet. Do as I have done."

John 13, verses 1 to 15

b

d

Something to think about:

Jesus wants us to look after and help each other, not push ourselves forward as if we are more important than other people.

Activity:

Which of the jug and bowl sets above did Jesus use in the big picture opposite?

Activity:

There are three things wrong with this trail. Can you circle the three footprints that are odd?

Prayer:

Dear God, help me to be kind to other people. What can I do to help someone today?

Judas kisses Jesus

Jesus went to the Garden of Gethsemane to pray. He knew that the time was soon coming when he would be arrested. Jesus needed his friends with him. He asked them to pray with him, but they were tired, and they kept falling asleep.

Suddenly, Judas Iscariot appeared. Behind him there was a noisy crowd brandishing swords and clubs.

Judas stepped forward and kissed Jesus on the cheek. It was a sign that one friend would give to another. But it was also a sign to the guards that this man was Jesus. Judas had betrayed his friend. The guards seized Jesus and took him away.

Mark 14, verses 43 to 46

Something to think about:

Why do you think Judas turned against Jesus?

Prayer:

Dear God, please help me to be a good friend and not turn against you as Judas did.

Activity:

Can you find the ten deliberate, crazy mistakes in the big picture? It should look like the picture below.

Peter's betrayal

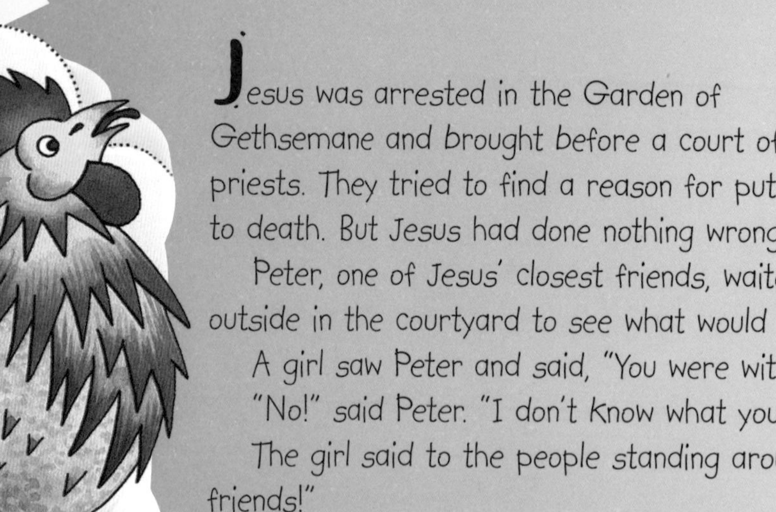

Jesus was arrested in the Garden of Gethsemane and brought before a court of chief priests. They tried to find a reason for putting him to death. But Jesus had done nothing wrong.

Peter, one of Jesus' closest friends, waited outside in the courtyard to see what would happen next. He was very afraid.

A girl saw Peter and said, "You were with Jesus, weren't you?"

"No!" said Peter. "I don't know what you're talking about!"

The girl said to the people standing around, "Look! He is one of Jesus' friends!"

"No I'm not!" said Peter.

Later, some other people recognised Peter and said, "You know Jesus!"

Again, Peter said he did not know Jesus.

Then he heard a rooster crow twice. He remembered something Jesus had said to him:

"Before a rooster crows twice, you will say three times that you do not know me at all."

Peter wept. He had betrayed his friend Jesus.

Mark 14, verses 66 to 72

Something to think about:

Would you stand up for Jesus if you were in Peter's place?

Activity:

How many times did the rooster crow? Join the red dots with just six lines to find out.

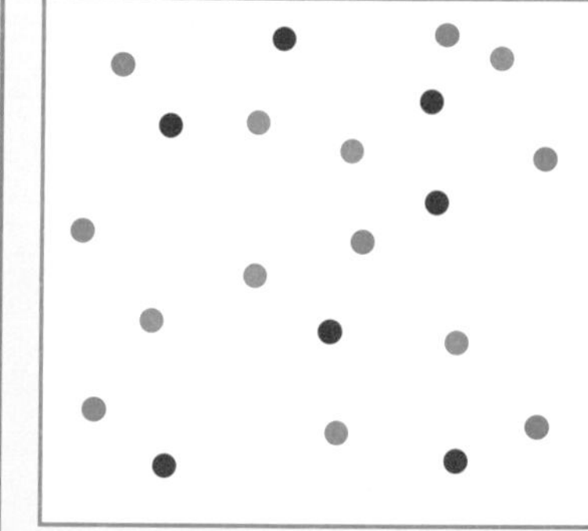

Activity:

Which of the six smaller roosters is the same as the large one?

Prayer: Dear God, help me to stand up for you, even when people tease me or say bad things.

Jesus cares for his mother

After Jesus' trial, he was taken away to be nailed to a cross. They crucified him, along with two thieves, on a hillside outside the city.

The soldiers who were watching took his clothes and shared them among themselves, but they gambled for his robe which was made from one piece of cloth.

Jesus' mother, Mary, stood nearby, weeping. Her sister was there too, and two other women who were his friends. Jesus looked from the cross and saw his friend John in the crowd. He spoke to his mother.

"Dear mother, here is your son," he said.

Then he spoke to John:

"Dear friend, here is your mother."

So John took Jesus' mother away to look after her in his home, just as Jesus wanted.

John 19, verses 25 to 27

Prayer:
Please help me always to think of others before myself.

Activity:

Color in the picture of John comforting Mary.

Mary was very upset. Can you draw a sad face?

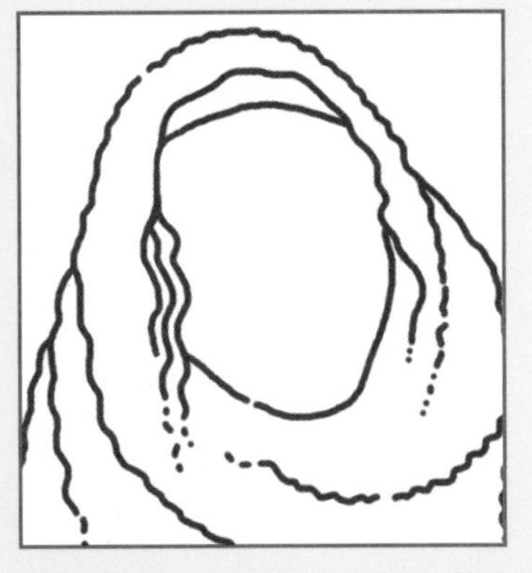

Something to think about:

Even when Jesus was in pain and dying, he thought of other people first.

Thomas believes

After Jesus had died, God raised him from death. The disciples all saw him – all except Thomas. Thomas did not believe Jesus could be alive again.

"Unless I see his hands and put my finger where the nails were hammered in, I shall not believe."

A week later, Thomas and some of Jesus' friends were together. All the doors were locked. Suddenly Jesus appeared there with them!

"Peace be with you!" said Jesus. Then he turned to Thomas. "Look at my hands. Put your finger in my wounds. Stop doubting and believe."

Thomas said, "My Lord and my God!" He worshipped Jesus.

"You have believed in me because you have seen me," said Jesus. "Happy are the people who believe even though they have not seen me."

John 20, verses 24 to 29

Something to think about:

What would you say to someone who can't believe Jesus is alive because they haven't seen him?

Prayer:

Dear God, thank you for helping us to believe Jesus is alive, even though we haven't seen him.

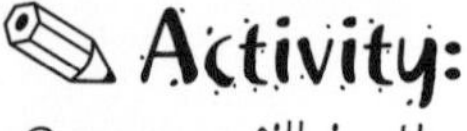

Activity:

Can you fill in the missing letters?

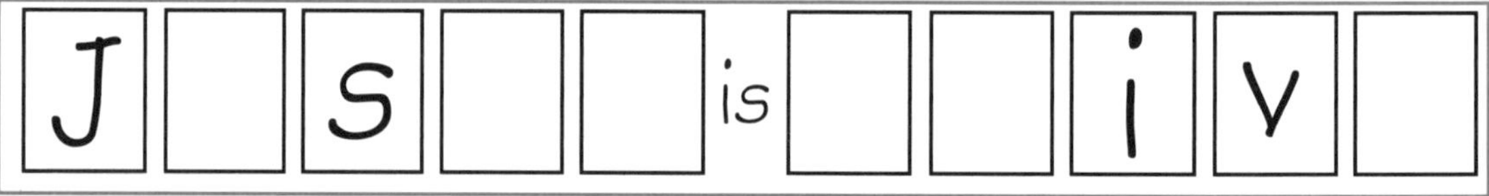

Activity:

Can you find the following ten words?

- [ ] JESUS
- [ ] WOUNDS
- [ ] DISCIPLES
- [ ] BELIEF
- [ ] THOMAS
- [ ] FAITH
- [ ] HANDS
- [ ] PEACE
- [ ] DOUBT
- [ ] HAPPY

					G	J	E	S	U	S
					D	P	E	H	R	C
					R	O	H	A	E	O
					E	Z	A	P	B	E
Q	T	D	I	S	C	I	P	L	E	S
W	H	A	N	D	S	F	P	P	L	W
A	O	R	D	N	Y	S	Y	E	I	O
R	M	W	O	U	N	D	S	A	E	U
B	A	I	U	J	J	F	W	C	F	N
Y	S	T	B	R	H	Y	N	E	O	D
F	A	I	T	H	Y	M	D	S	T	S

JESUS
THE TEACHER

Read, learn, pray, do the activities,
and find out more about what Jesus taught.

The wise and foolish builders

Something to think about:

How can we listen to Jesus?

Jesus once said:

"Anyone who listens to my words and does what I say is like a wise man who built his house upon a rock. The rain poured down, the wind blew hard, the rivers rose and tried to wash the house away. But the house didn't budge.

"But if you don't listen to what I say, you are like a foolish man who built his house upon the sand. The rain poured down, the wind blew hard, the rivers rose and tried to wash the house away. And the house fell down with an enormous CRASH!"

Luke 6, verses 47 to 49

Activity:

What two things do you need to do to be like the wise man?

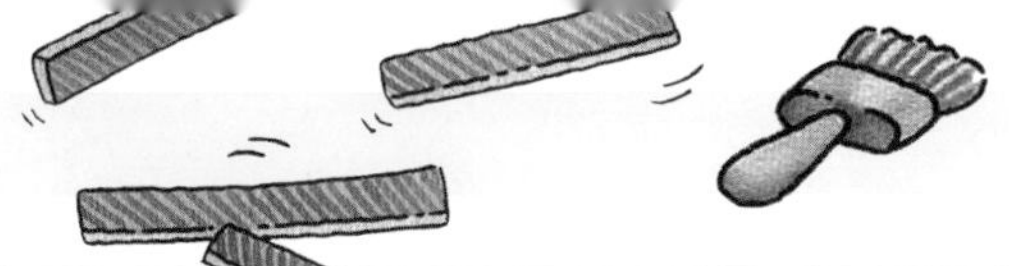

Activity:

Can you spot all ten differences between the pictures?

Prayer:

Dear God, help me to understand how to do the right things and live in a way that pleases you.

The hidden treasure

Jesus told another story about a man who found some treasure.

"Once a man found treasure hidden in a field. It was beautiful! It sparkled in the sunlight so that the man wanted to keep it. He covered it with earth again so that it was hidden in the ground.

"Then the man went away and sold everything that he had in the world, including his clothes, so that he could have enough money to buy the field. And by buying the field, he had also bought the treasure. Now the treasure belonged to him! He was really happy!"

Matthew 13, verse 44

Activity:

What color are these jewels?

Something to think about:

What is your greatest treasure?

Activity:

Connect the dots in the direction of the *black* lines to complete the picture.

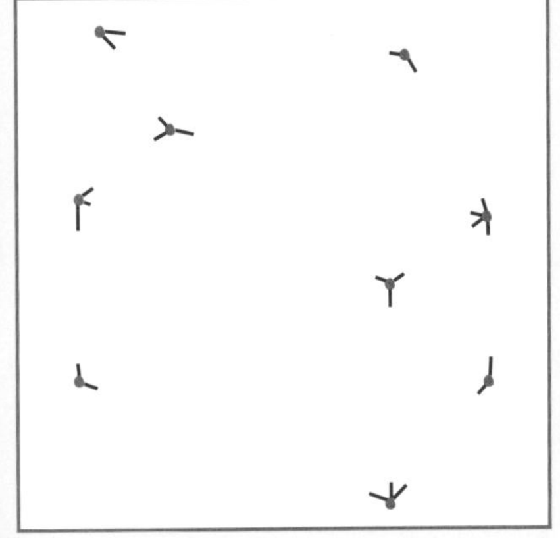

Prayer:

Dear God, help me to know that you are more important than anything else in the world.

The good Samaritan

Activity:
Can you find your way through the maze to help the injured man?

Jesus told this story to a man who asked how he could serve God best.

"One day, a man was travelling from Jerusalem to Jericho. Suddenly, a gang of robbers jumped out from behind a rock. They took all his money and clothes and hurt him badly.

Something to think about:
Are you a good friend to the people around you?

"The poor man lay in the road, unable to get up. Who could help him now?

"He heard the sound of footsteps. It was a priest. But the priest walked on by.

"Later on, a temple helper walked past, but he didn't stop either!

"The poor man in the road thought that now he really would die. But suddenly he heard more footsteps. It was a man from Samaria. He spoke kindly to the injured man, nursed his wounds, helped him on to his donkey and took him to an inn. He gave silver coins to the innkeeper to look after him."

Jesus asked, "Who acted as a neighbor to the injured man?"

"The one who helped him," replied the man.

"Go and do the same," said Jesus.

Luke 10, verses 30 to 37

Activity:
The man was on his way from where and where was he going?

J _ _ _ _ _ _ _ _

TO

_ _ _ _ _ _ O

Prayer:

Dear God, please help me to think of others and how I can help them.

A very greedy man

Jesus taught that it was not good to be greedy.

"There was once a man who was very rich. He was a farmer, so at first he stored all his crops in barns. When they became too full, he thought he would simply build bigger barns and enjoy all he had.

"He said to himself, 'Now I've stored up good things for many years. I'll eat, drink and take life easy.'

"But God spoke to him: 'You fool! Tonight your life will be taken from you. What good will all your riches be to you then?' "

Jesus said, "This is how it will be for people who keep all they have for themselves but do not think about God or other people."

Luke 12, verses 16 to 21

Something to think about:

What do you give to God?

Activity:

There are eleven coins hidden in the picture. Can you find eleven more coins hidden on these two pages?

Activity:
Can you find the eleven coins hidden in the picture?

Prayer:
Dear God, help me not to be greedy but to share what I have with others.

Activity:
How many coins are there all together?

Do not worry

Jesus told his disciples not to worry about food or clothes.

"Do not worry about your life," he said. "Life is more important than food, and the body is more important than clothes. Look at the ravens – God feeds them all. You are much more important than the birds. And look at the flowers of the field. They are more beautiful than a king's clothes! If that is how God clothes the flowers of the field, how much more will he look after you?

"Try to see how God wants you to live first, and God will give you everything you need."

Luke 12, verses 22 to 34

Something to think about:

What sort of things do you worry about easily?

Activity:

Can you find ten things in the word search that people worry about?

Prayer:

Dear God, thank you that you always look after me. Help me to trust you for everything I need.

Q S P I D E R S F R E T U

J O C O F J I R R S B S N

G M L S O E F Y I N C C D

H G O E O A E H E A L T H

O O T P D S D P N K I E R

S C H O O L L P D E F S E

T G E N E T O Y S S E W N

S O S Y J O B S A R O O A

The lost sheep

Jesus told a story about a shepherd who had a hundred sheep.

"The shepherd looked after each of his sheep. He made sure they had enough grass and fresh water and protected them from wild animals.

"One day the shepherd found that one was missing. So he set out to find his lost sheep, leaving the ninety-nine other sheep in the sheepfold.

"He looked high and low, behind bushes and rocks. Where could the sheep be?

"After some time, the shepherd heard faint bleating; it was the lost sheep! He picked it up lovingly and carried it home on his shoulders. He was so pleased to have found his lost sheep that he invited all his neighbors to a party.

"God is like that shepherd," said Jesus. "He cares even if only one of his sheep is lost."

Luke 15, verses 4 to 7

Something to think about:

Have you ever lost and found something very important to you?

Prayer:

Dear God, thank you that you always love me, even when I don't always follow you closely.

Activity:

Which track will lead to the lost sheep?

The loving father

There was a young man who lived on a farm with his family. He grew bored and wanted to go to the big city. So he asked his dad for his share of his riches and set off.

His father was very sad. He loved his son very much and hoped he would return.

The son spent all the money very quickly. But when the money ran out, nobody wanted to be his friend.

He had to find a job, feeding pigs. He was so hungry, he nearly ate the pigs' food. "I must go home," he thought. "Perhaps Dad will let me work on his farm."

As he came near to his old home, he saw his dad running towards him, shouting: "Welcome home!" The father gave a great party for his son. He thought he had lost him, but the son he loved had come back. How happy that made him!"

Luke 15, verses 11 to 32

Activity:

Join the dots to complete the picture.

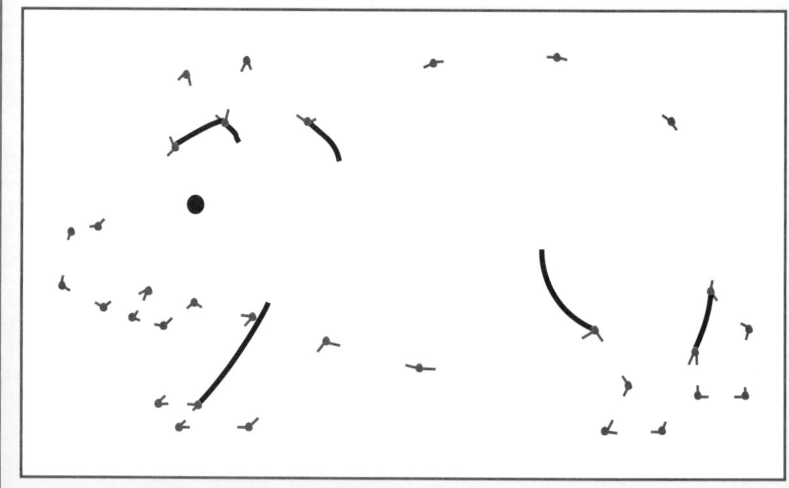

Don't forget to add a wiggly tail.

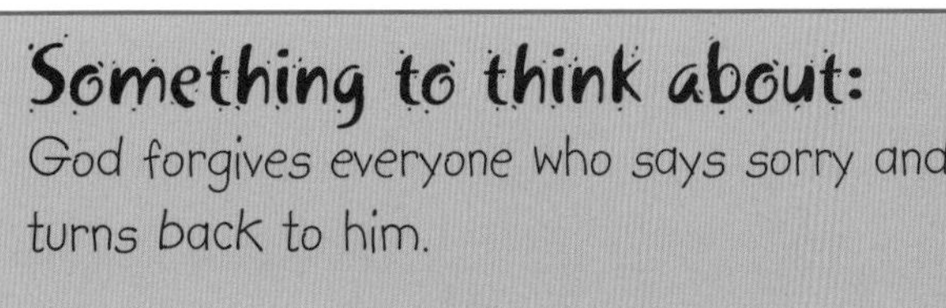

Something to think about:

God forgives everyone who says sorry and turns back to him.

Activity:

What did the father shout as his son returned?

Activity:

Can you count the pigs in the picture above?

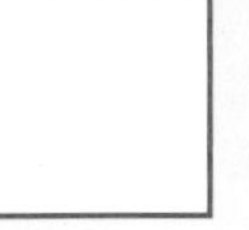

Prayer:

Dear God, I'm sorry for things I've done wrong today. I'm sorry that...

Two men at the temple

Jesus told this story to people who thought they were better than everyone else.

"One day two men went to the temple to pray to God.

"One man thought he was very good and prayed, 'Dear God, thank you that I am not greedy or a liar like other people. Thank you that I am not like that poor man over there. I pray to you at all the right times and give you just the right amount of my money.'

"The other man was not so pleased with himself. He prayed, 'Dear God,

I'm really sorry for all the things I've done wrong. Please forgive me.'

"The two men went home. God was pleased with the second man, not the first."

Luke 18, verses 9 to 14

Something to think about:

Why was God pleased with the second man?

Prayer:

Dear God, I'm sorry for the wrong things I do. Help me not to be proud or big-headed.

Activity:

Here are nine details taken from the big picture. Some copies are right, some have mistakes. Place the word "right" under the correct copies and the word "wrong" under the others.

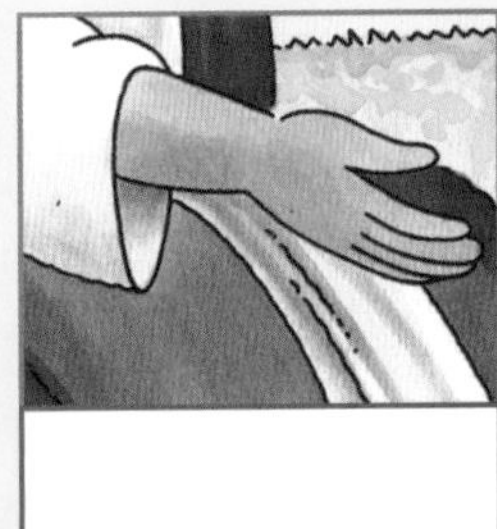

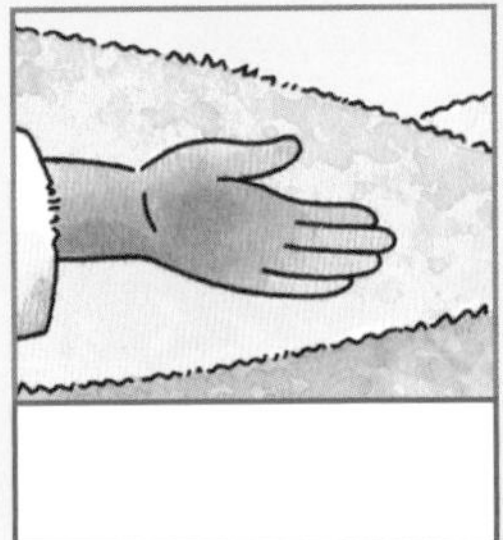

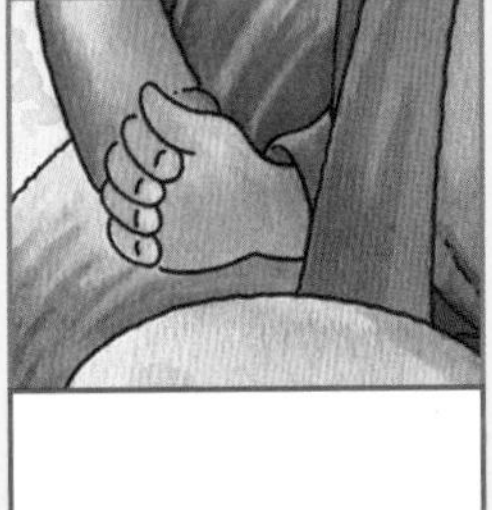

The rich young ruler

A rich young ruler asked Jesus, "What must I do to have eternal life?"

"Keep the ten commandments," said Jesus.

"I've kept them all my life," said the young man.

"Then there is one more thing," said Jesus. "Sell everything you have and give it all to the poor. Then come, follow me."

The young man was very sad, because he was very rich.

Jesus said, "It is very hard for rich people to enter God's kingdom. It is easier for a camel to go through the eye of a needle."

Luke 18, verses 18 to 30

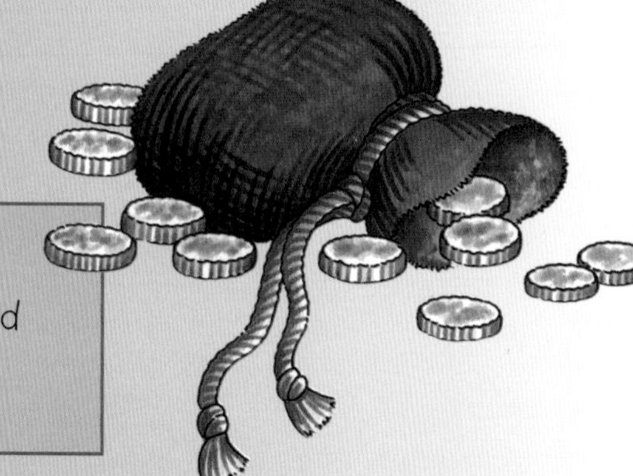

Something to think about:
If you were very rich, do you think you would find it hard to give all your money away?

Activity:

Can you color in the picture?

Activity:

The opposite of rich is poor. What is the opposite of the following?

Young

Sad

Easy

Prayer:

Dear God, help me to follow you first and not be greedy for fine things or money.

The widow's two coins

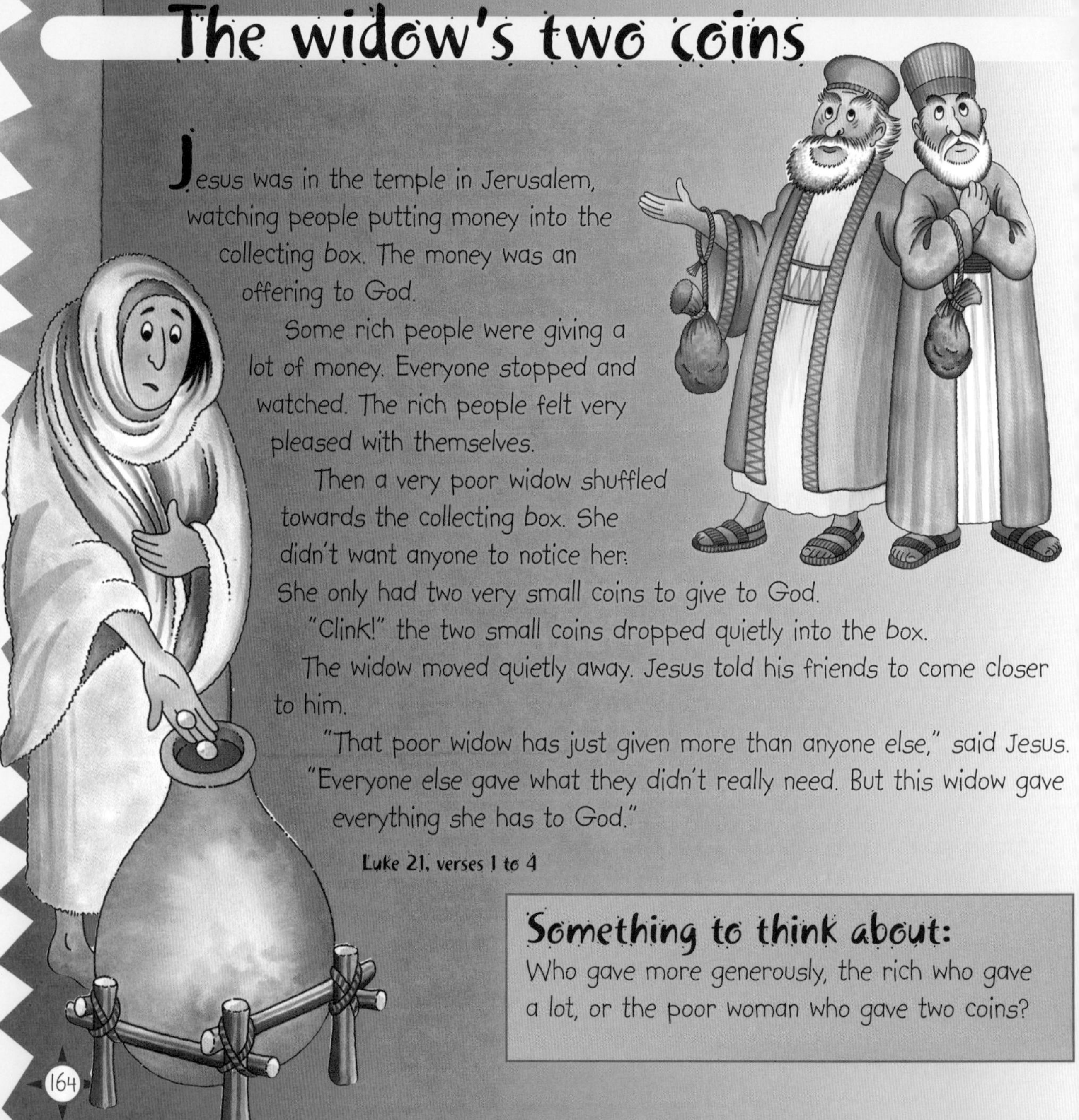

Jesus was in the temple in Jerusalem, watching people putting money into the collecting box. The money was an offering to God.

Some rich people were giving a lot of money. Everyone stopped and watched. The rich people felt very pleased with themselves.

Then a very poor widow shuffled towards the collecting box. She didn't want anyone to notice her. She only had two very small coins to give to God.

"Clink!" the two small coins dropped quietly into the box.

The widow moved quietly away. Jesus told his friends to come closer to him.

"That poor widow has just given more than anyone else," said Jesus. "Everyone else gave what they didn't really need. But this widow gave everything she has to God."

Luke 21, verses 1 to 4

Something to think about:

Who gave more generously, the rich who gave a lot, or the poor woman who gave two coins?

Activity:

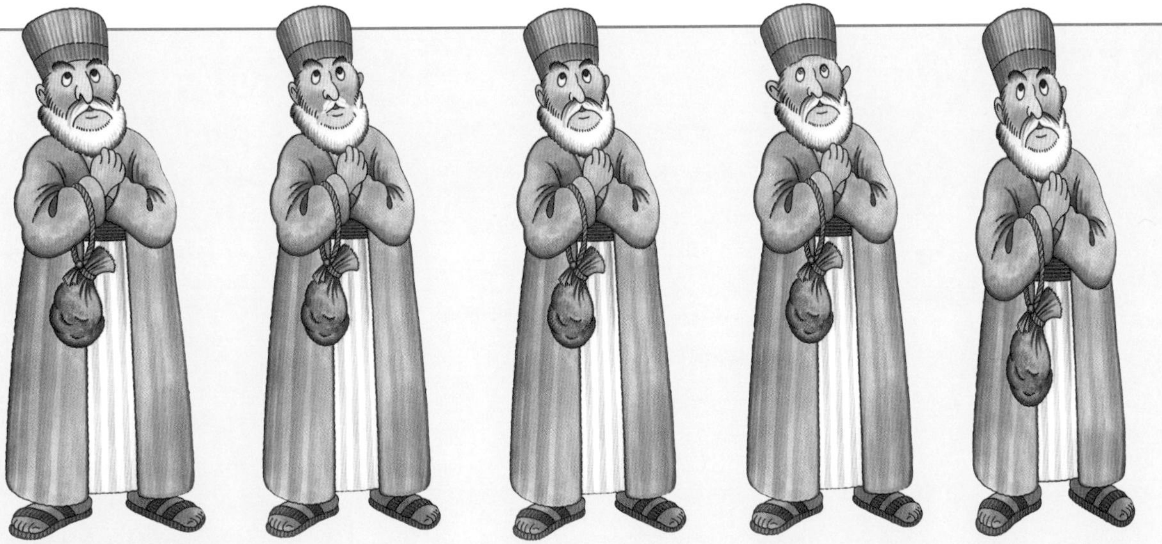

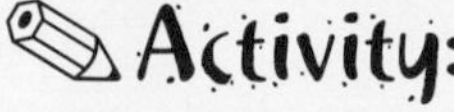

Which of these is the same rich man as pictured on the opposite page?

Prayer:

Dear God, thank you for all you give to me. Help me to give you everything.

Activity:

Can you complete this picture?

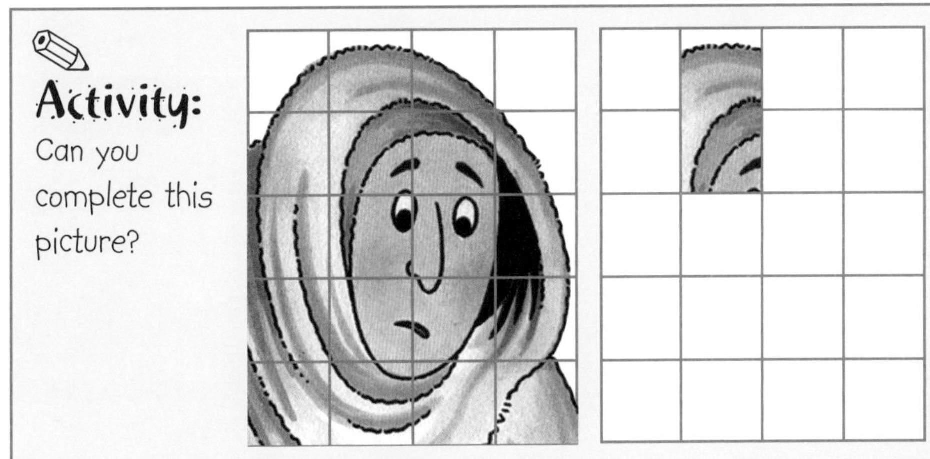

Living God's way

Jesus once spoke about the time he would come back to earth as King.

"The King will say to one group of people: 'The kingdom of heaven is ready for you. When I was hungry, you gave me food. When I was thirsty, you gave me a drink. You didn't know me, but your family welcomed me. You gave me clothes to wear. When I was ill, you looked after me. When I was in prison, you came to visit.' "

" 'When did we do that?' asked the people.

" 'When you did these things for anyone who needed help,' said the King, 'you did it for me.' "

Matthew 25, verses 31 to 45

Something to think about:

Why should we be kind to others?

Activity:

Draw an arrow from each circular detail to the same detail in the big picture.

Prayer:

Dear God, help me to notice when other people need help, and be kind to them, whoever they are.

Activity:

Draw an arrow to link each blue box to the right pink box.

When I was thirsty...	you gave me food.
When I was a prisoner...	you welcomed me.
When I was a stranger...	you gave me a drink.
When I was ill...	you visited me.
When I was hungry...	you gave me clothes to wear.
When I was cold...	you looked after me.

Activity:

What would you do to help?

When I was sad...	→	
When I was lost...	→	

JESUS DOES AMAZING THINGS

Read, learn, pray, do the activities, and find out about the amazing things Jesus did.

The wedding at Cana

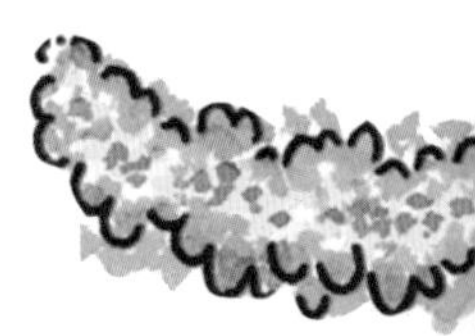

Jesus was invited to a wedding at Cana in Galilee.

There was a great feast and everyone was enjoying the party. Then suddenly the wine began to run out.

"Do something to help," said Mary, Jesus' mother.

Jesus knew what God wanted him to do. He told the servant to fill six large stone jars with water, then take them to the man in charge of the feast.

When the man tasted it, he was very pleased.

"Wonderful!" said the man. "People usually serve the best wine first, but you have left the best wine till last!"

He didn't know that Jesus had worked a miracle. Jesus had turned the water into wine!

John 2, verses 1 to 10

Something to think about:

Jesus can do amazing things if we ask him.

Prayer:

Dear God, thank you that you can make ordinary things special.

Activity:

How many jar handles can you see?

How many stone jars with the same red zig-zag pattern can you find?

A man with leprosy

Jesus went with his friends to a nearby town. They met a man there who had a terrible skin disease called leprosy. Nobody went near the man. He was very lonely and in pain. He hoped that Jesus could help him.

When the man saw Jesus coming, he threw himself at Jesus' feet, crying, "Lord, you can make me well again, if you want to."

Jesus put his hand on the man and said, "Yes, I do want to make you well. You are healed!"

All at once, the man's skin became normal and he was completely well again!

Jesus told him not to tell anyone about it, but to go to the priest.

"Show him that you are well again," said Jesus, "and offer a gift to God. Everyone will know that God has healed you."

News about what Jesus had done spread throughout the town.

Luke 5, verses 12 to 16

Something to think about:

Jesus asked the man to give a gift to God for making him well again. Do we remember to thank God when he answers our prayers?

Prayer:

Dear God,
help me to care about people who are ill. Help me to remember to ask you to help them.

Activity:

Can you see ten differences between the two pictures?

The soldier's servant

One day, a Roman officer came to Jesus for help.

"My servant is very ill," he said. "He is too ill to leave the house."

Jesus replied, "Then I will go to your house and make him well."

"No, no," said the officer. "I know how busy you are. But if you just say the word, I know he will be healed."

Jesus was surprised to hear this. He was pleased to find that the officer trusted him.

"Go home, then," said Jesus. "What you believe will be done."

The officer ran home. He found to his great joy that his servant had been made well again!

Luke 7, verses 1 to 10

Something to think about:

Is Jesus ever too busy to listen to us?

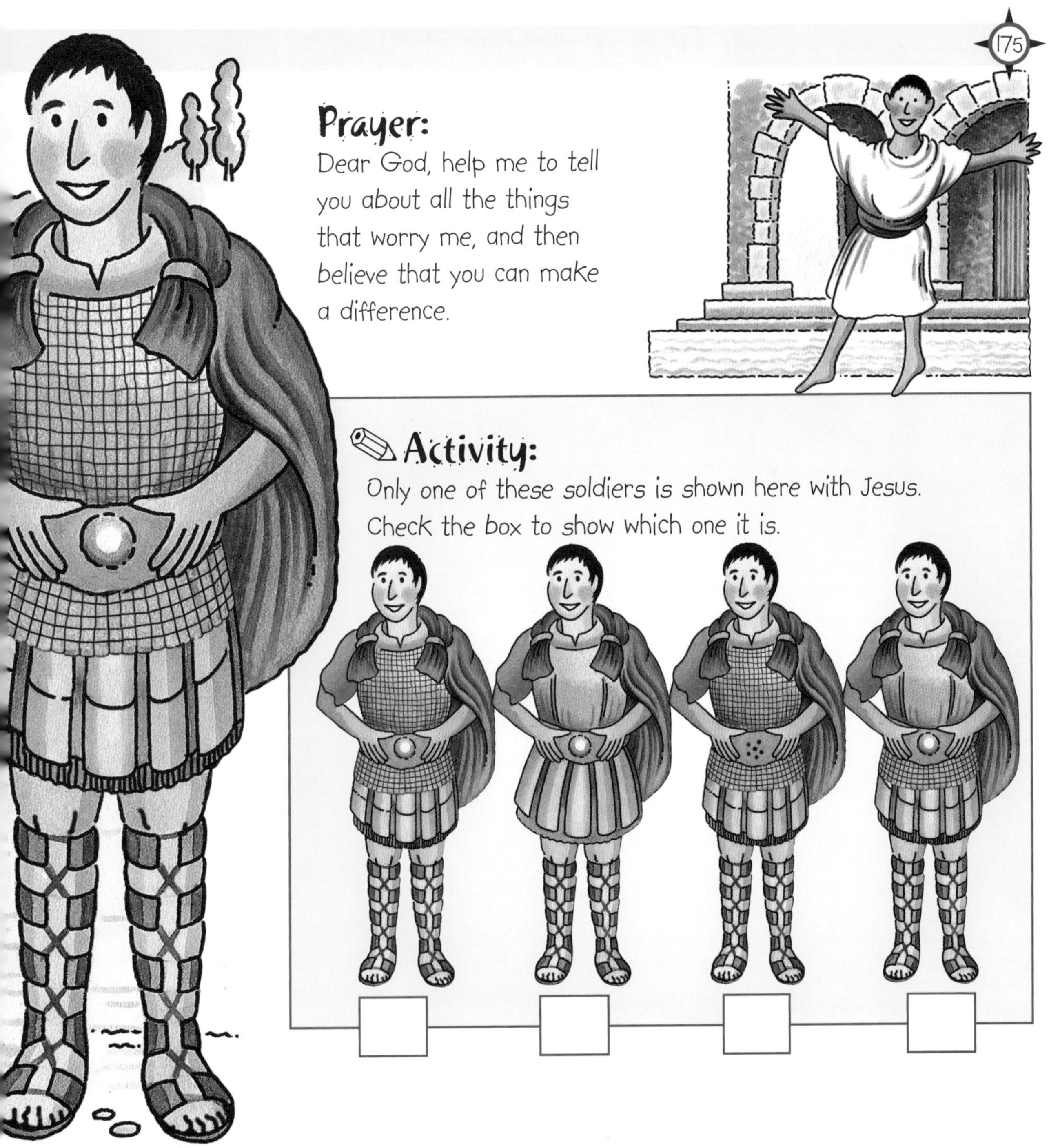

Prayer:

Dear God, help me to tell you about all the things that worry me, and then believe that you can make a difference.

Activity:

Only one of these soldiers is shown here with Jesus. Check the box to show which one it is.

Jesus helps a man to walk again

One day Jesus was speaking to a group of teachers of the Law, when some unexpected visitors arrived...

Jesus was inside a house talking to the teachers. There was a rustling noise above them and suddenly a large hole appeared in the ceiling!

Faces peered through the hole, and a mat was lowered down. On the mat lay a man who could not walk. His friends knew that Jesus could heal him. They could not bring him through the door because of all the crowds, so they had taken him up the stairs outside. They had thought of another way of getting in – by making a hole in the roof!

Jesus looked at the man kindly and said, "Your sins are forgiven."

The teachers grumbled – who did Jesus think he was? God himself?

Then Jesus said to the man, "Stand up! Pick up your mat and walk."

At once the man stood up and walked home, praising God for the amazing miracle which had happened.

Luke 5, verses 17 to 26

Something to think about:

The man's friends thought of an unusual way to reach Jesus. Can we help our friends to find him too?

Prayer:

Dear God, thank you for the friends who help us. Help me to be a special friend to people around me.

Activity:

These ropes are all tangled up. Can you tell how many ropes there are?

Activity:

Can you unscramble these words to find what the house roof was made of?

_ _ a _ _ _ _ s AND _ _ _

n a s h c r e b   m d u

Jesus makes a blind man see

One day people brought a blind man to Jesus. They wanted Jesus to make him see again.

Jesus walked with him out of the village. Then Jesus spat on the man's eyes and gently put his hands on them.

"Can you see anything yet?" asked Jesus.

"I can see some people, but they are all fuzzy, like trees walking around."

So Jesus put his hands on the man's eyes a second time. This time the man opened his eyes and could see perfectly! He was amazed to see the colorful world and the kind face of Jesus.

"Go home now," said Jesus, "but don't go back to the village."

Mark 8, verses 22 to 26

Something to think about:

Hold your hands over your eyes and imagine being blind. Now lift them off and imagine how the blind man felt when he could see again.

Prayer:

Dear God, thank you that you can change people's lives.

_ _ _

_ _ _ e _

_ a _ _ _ _

_ _ _ b

_ _ e _

Activity:

Can you see what each of these silhouettes is?

Jesus calms a storm

One day, Jesus and his friends got into a boat on the lake. It had been a very busy day and Jesus was tired.

Suddenly a fierce storm blew up. The boat was rocked about like a cork, and the waves splashed over the side. The disciples were terrified of sinking. But Jesus was fast asleep.

"Save us, Lord!" they shouted to Jesus.

"Why are you so afraid?" said Jesus, waking up.

Then Jesus got up and ordered the wind and the waves to calm down.

The storm vanished. Everyone was amazed!

"Even the wind and the waves obey him!" they said.

Jesus had saved his friends from drowning in the storm.

Luke 8, verses 22 to 25

Something to think about:

Jesus' friends were with him all the time, but even they didn't understand that he had power over the natural world.

Prayer:

Help me to talk to you when I am afraid, Lord God. Please be there to take away my fears.

Activity:

Find two words below that describe each of the following:

☐ ☐ Jesus

☐ ☐ The weather

☐ ☐ The disciples

Q	W	I	C	D	Y	F	C	T
W	S	T	O	R	M	Y	W	I
A	S	L	E	E	P	M	I	R
R	Y	R	N	W	Z	F	N	E
S	B	A	M	A	Z	E	D	D
Y	D	D	J	Y	E	K	Y	U
T	E	R	R	I	F	I	E	D
M	R	T	A	J	S	O	N	P
A	E	S	G	H	I	O	P	B

Jesus feeds a hungry crowd

Jesus was once speaking to a large crowd of people. There were men, women and even children. They had been listening to him all day and were getting hungry.

Jesus' friends thought the people should go away and buy some food, but Jesus wanted to feed them.

"Where can we buy food for all these people?" he asked his friends.

Philip replied, "We would need more than two hundred silver coins to buy enough!"

Andrew, another of Jesus' friends, said, "There is a boy who says he will share his lunch. But he has only five rolls and two small fishes."

But then Jesus did something amazing! He thanked God for the food, then shared it out among everyone!

No one went away hungry. Jesus gave them all enough to eat, and there were even twelve baskets full of left-overs.

John 6, verses 1 to 13

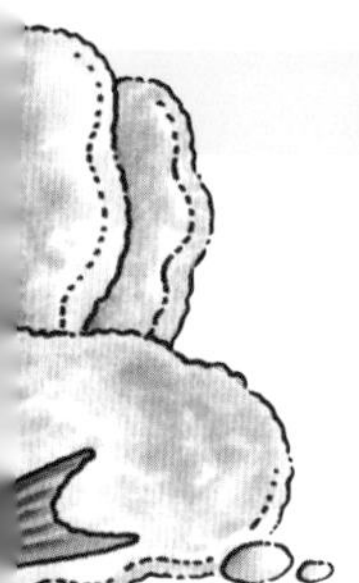

Something to think about:

Jesus accepts even the small amount we offer him and does great things with it.

Prayer:

Help me, Lord God, to share all that I have with those around me.

Activity:

After everyone had eaten, there were still many *baskets* of food left over. How many *baskets* can you count?

Jesus walks on the water

After Jesus had fed the crowds, his friends went down to the lake where they found a boat. They set off across the lake for Capernaum. Jesus was not with them.

A stormy wind blew up and the water on the lake became choppy. The men kept on rowing but were rather scared.

Suddenly, they saw Jesus coming towards them. He was walking on the water! They couldn't believe what they saw and were very afraid.

"Don't be frightened," said Jesus. "You all know me – your friend, Jesus."

They wanted him to come aboard. At once the boat reached the shore, and they were all safe.

John 6, verses 16 to 21

Something to think about:
How could Jesus walk on the water?

Prayer:

Dear God, help us to remember that Jesus can do more than we can ever imagine.

___ ___ e

___ o ___ ___

___ ___ a ___

___ ___ c ___

Activity:

Lots of things can float on water, but only Jesus could walk on water. Can you join the dots to complete the pictures and name the things that float?

Jesus heals Jairus' daughter

One day Jesus was asked to help a man called Jairus whose daughter was dying. Was there anything Jesus could do? Jairus loved his daughter so much. If only Jesus could reach her in time...

But there were huge crowds around Jesus and a woman came forward to touch Jesus' cloak. She had been ill for years, and Jesus healed her. It was a wonderful day for her.

Suddenly a messenger from Jairus' house came with some dreadful news. Jairus' daughter was dead.

"Don't be afraid," said Jesus. "Believe, and she will be healed."

They hurried to Jairus' house and Jesus saw the girl who was dead. Everyone was weeping and wailing with sadness.

Jesus held the girl's hand and said, "Get up, my child!"

The girl came back to life and stood up!

"Give her some food," said Jesus to her parents. "She's hungry."

They were amazed at what Jesus had done and overjoyed to have their little girl back again.

Luke 8, verses 40 to 56

Prayer:

Dear God, help me to keep on trusting you when I find something difficult. Thank you that you hear my prayers.

Activity: Color in this picture.

Something to think about:

Everyone had given up hope that Jairus' daughter would be saved. But Jesus came to the rescue!

The healing at the pool

There was a pool in Jerusalem called Bethesda. Many people who couldn't walk or see used to lie there, hoping to be healed when the water in the pool was stirred up.

Jesus came to the pool and saw a man who had been unable to walk for thirty-eight years.

"Do you want to get well?" Jesus asked him.

"I have no one to help me into the pool," replied the man. "Someone else always gets there first."

Jesus said to the man, "Get up! Pick up your mat and walk!"

The water hadn't

stirred in the pool. But Jesus had healed the man. He could walk again!

John 5, verses 1 to 9

Prayer:

Dear God, thank you that Jesus did amazing miracles and can still help people today.

Something to think about:

What do you think you'd do first if you could walk again after thirty-eight years?

Activity:

Can you answer these questions about other people that Jesus healed?
Write the answers in the boxes provided.

This man described people as fuzzy what?

Whose daughter is this?

What did Jesus ask her parents to give her?

What did this man suffer from?

What did this disease affect?

This man entered the room through...?

Jesus said, "Pick up your mat and... ."

The amazing catch of fish

After Jesus was crucified, God raised Jesus from the dead. The stone was rolled away from Jesus' tomb and Jesus came back to life.

One of the first times that Jesus was seen again by his friends was when Jesus did another amazing thing...

Jesus' friends were fishing on the lake, but they had caught nothing all night. Early in the morning, they saw a man on the shore.

"Throw your nets on the right side of the boat, and you will catch plenty of fish!" shouted the man.

They did as he told them, and at once their nets were filled with so many fish that they could not pull the nets back into the boat!

Peter, Jesus' dear friend, knew at once that the man on the shore must be Jesus!

He jumped into the water and ran joyfully to Jesus. Jesus was alive again!

John 21, verses 1 to 14

Something to think about:

Peter knew that Jesus was alive because he saw him.

How can we find out more about Jesus?

Prayer:

Dear God, thank you that Jesus is alive and that we can know him too.

Activity:

There are five things wrong with this picture. Can you spot them all?

Hendrickson Publishers, Inc.
P. O. Box 3473
Peabody, Massachusetts 01961-3473

ISBN 1-59856-042-5

Hendrickson Edition First Printing—August 2006

Editorial Director Annette Reynolds
Art Director Gerald Rogers
Pre-production Krystyna Hewitt
Production John Laister

Printed and bound in China